赵琛 著

中国建筑工业出版社
CHINA ARCHITECTURE & BUILDING PRESS

福陵

世界文化遗产 辽宁卷

WORLD HERITAGE
LIAONING VOLUME
FULING IMPERIAL
TOMB

罗哲文收赵琛为入门弟子
Professor Luo Zhewen accepted Zhao Chen as his apprentice

序言——星星之火

我对关外"一宫三陵"非常了解，当年申遗时，我还提议，三陵不可分割，以扩展项目参与申遗，并一举成功。当前我国古建研究面临的现状，建筑专业很少开课，古建技术即将失传，那些既是艺术家又是工人的建筑研究者们，后继无人。古建筑是凝固的历史，一个没有历史的民族就好比一个人失去了记忆，我多么希望后辈学者能够接过先师与我手中的尺笔，好好保护祖国几千年遗留下来的那些古建筑遗产。

当年，赵琛拿着厚厚的一摞书稿，以"愿乞一言以托不朽"的谦虚与诚恳的态度邀我为他作序，我内心生出万千感慨，也产生了很重的责任感。而这次，是我第三次为他写序言了，写他家乡的遗产。赵琛以家乡人的角度去看世界文化遗产，当然比其他人更多一份了解，更多一份感情，也更多一份权威。他始终站在全局的角度，客观描述历史，尤其是对清代帝王陵寝学的研究，将整个清代陵寝作为一个体系，不孤立不分割，横向对比，纵向研究，可谓独树一帜。很多人都了解自己家乡，自己周围的事，却不能了解全局，赵琛恰恰能做到既了解家乡，又了解全局，"知己知彼"。清代陵寝的保护工作也没有做到这样，几乎陵与陵之间都是单独个体，甚至没有联系，没有整体意识，对文物的保护也是相当不利的。赵琛的这种思维，给我们一种思考，一种关于文化遗产保护的整体思考。关于中国的文物保护工作，不是各自顾各自，也不是一个人单打独斗能够完成的。

赵琛，一个人能够二十余年，锲而不舍，持之以恒地做一件事，可以说是很了不起的，尤其是古建筑研究并没有经济上的收入。只摄影一项，就需要大量的金钱投入，有人说："想让谁破产，就送他照相机"。现在的时代，是金钱时代，一些年轻人赚来的钱，都用于享受生活了。没有钱的工作，没人愿意干。然而就算一个人有足够的资金，也未必有这样的时间和兴趣。据我了解，赵琛这个人没什么嗜好，赚来的钱都花在古建研究上和摄影上了。很多人不理解赵琛，然而我理解。可能是因为他是学美术的，所以对美学很有研究，因此在摄影上他比其他人更懂得审美和构图，加上他有胆识，有见识，更有猎人一样的耐力和精准的洞察力，使他在摄影上的造诣远非一般人能及。每次见到他，我的内心都会想到那句古话，所谓"天将降大任于斯人也"。

"德成而上，艺成而下"，赵琛却可以说是德艺双馨了，出类拔萃，是同代学者中的佼佼者。七十年间，我研究古建筑，照片和摄影集看多了，只有文字的考察报告也看了很多，都觉枯燥，没什么新意。这本书却以独特的视觉，集摄影、绘画、文字于一体，摄影作品精彩，绘画生动真实，文字通俗易懂，三者结合，而治学态度严谨，书中甚至指出了申遗时测绘不准确的地方。曹雪芹写红楼，十年辛苦不寻常，赵琛却用二十余年时间做古建研究，时间的累积，阅历的丰富，知识的广博，其著作的内容和水平，同类书籍实难比肩。此外，全书还蕴涵了深厚的民族情感，对古建研究的未来的担忧，对历史文化传承的发扬，对后来人的培养与关注。作者始终站在历史的角度，纵观全局，将自己的渺小融于热爱的古建研究中去，不拘泥于个人，不局限于时代，体现出一种无私的大爱与博爱。再次为赵琛作序，我深觉缘分匪浅，他以一己之力，力撑古建这座欲将倾颓之厦，使我在耄耋之年，总算看到了一点希望，"星星之火，期以燎原"，同时也对他在学术上有如此硕果而深表祝贺。

PREFACE — SPARKS OF FIRE

When Professor Zhao Chen invited me with an unpretentious sincerity to draw up a preface for his newly crafted manuscript under the pretext of "soliciting a word for the honor of eternity," my heart was overcome with strong emotions, sensing a heavy burden of responsibility as well. This is my third time to write a preface for his works on legacies of his hometown.

I know quite well about "the Imperial Palace and Three Imperial Mausoleums" outside Shanhai Pass. I proposed then to combine the three mausoleums as an integral extended part in the application for World Heritage, and fortunately succeeded at one stroke. Currently, ancient Chinese architecture research is confronted with multifold problems, for instance, few ancient architecture courses are lectured, ancient architectural techniques are not being handed down and none is willing to inherit the craftsmanship of those architecture researchers who are both artists and architects. Ancient architecture is more or less like cemented and solidified history, and a nation without history is like a man with no memory. How I wish that the younger people could take over the historic task of preserving the legacy of our ancient architecture handed down through thousands of years. Professor Zhao Chen examines the world heritage from a perspective of a local scholar, which helps ensure a better understanding with a touch of emotion and a tinge of authority. He always stands on a global position so that he can see the panorama clearly and describe history objectively. He has done a spectacular job in his study of imperial mausoleums of Qing Dynasty, at which he looks as an integral system with methods of horizontal contrast and longitudinal researches. Many people know about their hometown and things around, but few understand things as a whole. However, Zhao Chen is one of the few who boast of holoscopic insights regarding mausoleums both in hometown and throughout China. The protection of Qing mausoleums faces a dilemma, i.e. each mausoleum is protected separately without due consideration of preserving them as a whole, which is undoubtedly detrimental to heritage protection. What Zhao Chen has done ignites the introspection concerning the conundrum of how to carry out the nationwide cultural heritage preservation and protection, for a sound solution can't be guaranteed by relying merely on individual or separate efforts.

Professor Zhao Chen can be crowned with the wreath of greatness for his more-than-twenty-years unremitting perseverance in his study of ancient architecture, and, in particular, for the fact that it brings no economic returns. Take photography for example, it consumes a large amount of money, and a saying goes like this, "If you want someone to go bankrupt, send him a camera." In an era of hot materialist pursuit when some young people dissipate their earnings, no job can arouse much attention or attraction if it brings no money at all. Even a person who is well off may have no time or think it uninteresting to study ancient architecture. As far as I know, Zhao Chen is attached to nothing but ancient architecture study and photography, in which he spends extravagantly. Many people probably don't understand why, but I can understand his devotion. He majored in art with deep understanding of aesthetics, so he knows better the beauty and composition of photography. In addition, with his courage and knowledge, single-minded stamina, and accurate insights, he has made great achievements in photography that common people couldn't match. Every time I lay my eyes on him, a saying naturally jumps out into my mind, "God is about to place great responsibilities on this man."

"The achievement in virtue is held to be of superior worth, and the accomplishment of art in the next place." Professor Zhao Chen, one of the top scholars, can be acclaimed to be eximious in his quest of both virtue and art. In the course of ancient architecture study for the last seventy years, I have seen plenty of photos and albums and read a good many of tedious plain reports, most of which are humdrum and boring. But this book has a unique vision presented through combining photography, drawing and text. Wonderful photography, vivid drawing, easy-to-understand text, plus Zhao's rigorous attitude in the study, all these features make the book outstanding. The minor mistake made in surveying and mapping in application for World Cultural Heritage well illustrates Zhao's preciseness with facts and figures. It took ten years of extraordinary hardship for Cao Xueqin to finish the classic Dream of Red Mansions, while the study of ancient architecture cost Zhao over twenty years of his life. The author's timeless efforts, rich experience, extensive knowledge, and unique content of the book make this book unparalleled. What's more, his strong patriotism, his love and anxiety for ancient architecture, his concerns over passing down and cultivating a love for historical and cultural heritage could be sensed between lines of this book. Zhao always takes a historical perspective and devotes himself to the study of ancient architecture without considering individual welfare or limitation of his time, which demonstrates his selflessness and broadmindedness. I do feel it a great honor, at my ripe age, to write a few words for Zhao's book again, and want here to extend my heart-felt congratulations on his academic achievements. His devotion and commitment to ancient Chinese architecture and culture kindles my hope in preserving and resurrecting ancient Chinese culture, believing "a little spark can start a prairie fire."

目 录 CONTENTS

序言——星星之火
PREFACE—SPARKS OF FIRE

仁者乐山 / 6
THE BENEVOLENT FIND JOYS IN HILLS / 8

中国的陵寝学 / 11
MAUSOLEUM CULTURE IN CHINA / 12

为何定名为福陵？ / 14
WHY NAMED AS FULING IMPERIAL TOMB? / 15

官员至此下马 / 16
OFFICIALS DISMOUNT HERE / 17

失去下马功能的牌坊 / 20
PAIFANG: LOSING THE FUNCTION OF DISMOUNTING / 23

正红门的学问 / 27
ENIGMA OF FRONT RED GATE / 29

琉璃龙壁上的工名 / 30
SIGNATURE OF CRAFTSMEN ON GLAZED COILED DRAGON WALL / 34

粗犷的华表 / 37
BOLD AND UNSTRAINED HUABIAO / 38

罕见的老虎石象生 / 41
RARE TIGER STONE STATUES / 45

灵魂之道——神道 / 48
SPIRIT PATH / 48

使人卑躬屈膝的神桥 / 51
SPIRIT BRIDGE, WHICH ONE HAS TO BOW WHEN CROSSING ON IT / 53

清陵独一的一百单八蹬 / 56
BEST PLACE OF FULING IMPERIAL TOMB – 108 STEPS / 56

退役的神龟 / 58
RETIRED DIVINE TURTLE / 60

神碑幻影 / 63
PHANTOMS OF DIVINE STELE / 64

福陵祭祀 / 67
FULING IMPERIAL TOMB SACRIFICE / 70

清代帝陵独有的方城 / 74
SQUARE CITY, A UNIQUE BUILDING OF QING MAUSOLEUMS / 77

羊角神兽隆恩门 / 79
EMINENT FAVOR GATE WITH A GOAT-HORN DIVINE ANIMAL / 80

摄影的最佳视点——角楼 / 89
TURRET — IDEAL SPOT OF PHOTO-TAKING / 90

为太祖帝后灵魂居住的隆恩殿 / 96
EMINENT FAVOR HALL: RESTING PLACE FOR TAI TSU (EMPEROR HONG TAIJI) AND HIS EMPRESS / 101

努尔哈赤的圣德神功 / 103
VIRTUES AND DEEDS OF GREAT NURHACI / 106

建州与叶赫的爱恨情仇 / 108
LOVE AND HATE BETWEEN JIANZHOU AND YEHE / 110

为何用亲生子女联姻 / 112
IMMEDIATE RELATIVES FOR INTERMARRIAGE / 113

帝后灵魂暂居的东配殿 / 114
EAST SIDE-HALL WHERE SPIRIT OF EMPRESS RESIDES / 114

为喇嘛诵经建的西配殿 / 116
WEST SIDE-HALL BUILT FOR SUTRAS CHANTING / 116

阴阳两界的邮局——焚帛亭 / 118
POST OFFICE BETWEEN LIFE AND DEATH — SILK-BURNING PAVILION / 120

人无路，魂有道的二柱门 / 122
DUAL PILLAR DOOR WHERE SPIRIT ENTERS AND EXITS / 122

皇帝举哀之处——石五供 / 125
EMPEROR MOURNING PLACE — STONE FIVE OFFERINGS / 126

雷火中永生的大明楼 / 129
GRAND MING TOWER, SURVIVAL FROM THUNDER AND LIGHTNING / 133

月牙城还是哑巴院？ / 136
CRESCENT CITY OR DUMB'S COURTYARD / 139

十一与福陵风水 / 140
NUMBER 11 AND GEOMANCY OF FULING IMPERIAL TOMB / 140

宝顶里葬有几位妃子？ / 142
HOW MANY CONCUBINES WERE BURIED IN BLESSED VAULT / 144

大妃阿巴亥是自愿殉葬吗？ / 147
PRINCIPAL CONCUBINE ABAHAI: IS SHE WILLING TO BE BURIED ALIVE WITH EMPEROR? / 148

神榆与大清的命运 / 150
DIVINE ELM AND FATE OF GREAT QING DYNASTY / 153

站班的古松也是文物 / 155
GUARDIAN PINES ARE ALSO ANTIQUITY / 157

卧虎藏龙 / 158
CROUCHING TIGERS AND HIDDEN DRAGONS / 161

天赐的紫气东来 / 163
BLESSED PURPLE AIR COMING FROM THE EAST / 163

结语——四十五年分之一秒 / 164
EPILOGUE — ONE SECOND OUT OF 45 YEARS / 166

注解 / 170
NOTES / 172

天柱山麓／下图
Foot of Mount Tianzhu / Lower

仁者乐山

沈阳周遭几乎没有山，所以从小时候起，我就对山特别向往。沈阳的山很少也都很小，记忆里小时候只去过一次棋盘山。自从姥姥给我讲了家族的历史，祖上世代守陵，我就常常去天柱山周围。在这座山脚下，安静地沉睡着一代帝王的英魂，这就是大清王朝的开拓者努尔哈赤的陵寝——福陵。福陵，因地处沈阳东郊，故沈阳人又称之为东陵。

福陵，前临浑河，背靠辉山、天柱山，两山之间还有一条兴隆岭。不过，正所谓"山不在高，有'陵'则名"。天柱山，因为有了福陵，而成为沈阳独特的风景。

福陵对我来说，一直是个神秘而亲切的地方，却没有机会走近。十二岁那年，少年宫组织夏令营活动，其中一天的安排是去东陵公社采摘山里红，我心里很激动。路过福陵的正红门广场休息时，我还用车辙坑里的水画了一张正红门的画，无奈大门紧闭，无从知晓红墙里边是什么模样。福陵，在我的心目中就更加神秘了。

十七岁我约了两个少年宫的伙伴，带上速写本去福陵，当年路途非常遥远，坐车就需要半天时间，天黑前必须回来，所以只在陵寝里匆匆画了几张。直到考大学前，我还经常在前陵堡画速写，只是一直没有机会进到红墙里面去。十九岁考大学那年，姥姥说如果我考上了，就奖励我一架相机，虽然第一年我落榜了，不过姥姥还是送给我一架相机，她鼓励我明年再考。第二年我如愿考上了鲁迅美术学院。爸爸的几位学生邀请我们全家出去郊游，让我选地方，我毫不犹豫地说："东陵"。那是我第一次真正亲眼看到福陵的全貌，并深深为之震撼。那次郊游勾起了我以后学习、研究和走上保护古建筑之路的最初冲动，成为我人生中重要的一课。此后不论是我前进的途中有了收获的喜悦，还是遇到坎坷艰辛，我都会去福陵转转，按动快门的刹那便是"忘我"，每次耗尽胶卷，才感到疲惫，这是我唯一的健身方式吧！

我从十二岁游学开始，爬吕山、登泰山，走遍了祖国的三山五岳，发现所有的山都比沈阳天柱山高，就连棋盘山的海拔都在一千米以上，而天柱山的海拔最高处仅两百多米，我不禁思索，为什么清朝皇帝会把努尔哈赤的陵寝选在天柱山？悟了很多年，后来研究才知道，古代选择陵址有"前有照，后有靠""风水"学问，即要依山临水，也有一种说法是"两山夹一岗，辈辈出皇上"。而福陵，正符合上述条件，是一块千古难寻的风水宝地。风水学中也有，山者龙也之说，而有山必有水，所谓"有山无水休寻地"，福陵前有一个龙滩，据说是浑河流经多年冲积而成的小沙滩，弥补了风水学中的有山无水的缺憾。而天柱山经清帝王保护，岁月流转，在沈阳人心中早已成为一块圣地，它在人心中的高度，远远高于它的实际海拔，在这里的高度，已不是科学概念，而是人文概念，是一种精神，是大清的精神支柱。而我一直想把天柱山拍下来，最初围着福陵走，却怎么也没发现山在哪。后来在西边一处，看到了一个高点的土坡。我猜想这应该就是天柱山了吧，也就真的只有一两百米的海拔。三百多年来，人们自发地保护着这片土地，如今在前陵堡的村落中，仍然住着很多当年看守福陵的人的后代，如：肇、赵、那、贺、赫、西等姓氏。他们都是满族人，只是很多已经被汉化了。

孔子曰："仁者乐山。"（注解1）古代帝王陵寝选址、规划也主要受儒家"天人合一"思想的影响，认为天是赋予人仁义礼智本性的存在。在努尔哈赤长达27个字的谥号中，就有一个仁字，而福陵，也恰恰体现出了仁者乐山的一面。仁者，安于义理，仁慈宽容而不易冲动，性情就像山一样稳重不迁，所以用山来形容。努尔哈赤，一生戎马倥偬，从未停止过征伐，很多人难免质疑，甚至有人认为他残暴，争论一直未曾停止。很多开国君主的残暴，有诸多因素，更是无奈之举。秦始皇焚书坑儒，却不失为一伟大始皇帝，汉武帝晚年，相信巫蛊，杀戮太过，却也不失为一代明君。相反，南唐李后主的仁，却导致了亡国。努尔哈赤的仁，不是妇人之仁，而是大仁大义。忠义仁勇化身的关羽，就是努尔哈赤生前最为推崇的正义之神。很多人都想成为仁者，然而真正成为仁者的人却很少，成为大仁者更是凤毛麟角。福陵及其建筑，却在无声中诠释了努尔哈赤的仁，正是这种帝王之仁，才使后人对它尊崇膜拜，使之与天地同，与山水融，成为一种精神标志。保护福陵，就必须保护福陵的山，山是福陵建筑的组成部分，也是世界文化遗产的组成部分。

我带着默默诠释精神的信仰，对福陵内心生出一种偏爱。我从最初的画，到后来的集中拍摄，至少已有20年了。从1998年开始，我每年都要对福陵进行一次集中拍摄，照片里留下了很多珍贵的资料，而比资料更珍贵的是记忆。很多人都说福陵的规制比昭陵小，但是，这并不影响福陵在我心中的神圣。永陵、福陵、昭陵，盛京三陵，加上已列入世界遗产名录的清东陵、清西陵，不仅构成了一组清帝陵体系，更是一部浓缩了的清朝历史。它们如同申遗时一样，可以说是一个不可分割的整体，研究其中任何一座陵寝，都不能孤立地去看，而必须站在整个体系基础上。只是这整体中的局部，在我心中的位置，各有千秋。

可能，每个人心中都有一片山林、一片净土，以求心灵的归隐。漫步在福陵的百年古松间，眼见碧水萦绕，青山如墨，万松叠翠，我的内心也多了一份宁静，一份喜悦。

于山外堂

THE BENEVOLENT FIND JOYS IN HILLS

There are almost no mountains around Shenyang, a city in northeast China. From my childhood, I have been longing for seeing mountains. There are hills, but few and small. In my memory, the only hill I paid visit to is Mount Qipan. Since I was quite acquainted by my grandma with the long history of the nearby mausoleum protection passed down on from the ancestors of my mother's family, I began visiting here and there around Mount Tianzhu now and then. Mount Tianzhu, as its name indicates, gives me a feeling that it looks like a heaven supporting pillar. At the foot of the mountain, a stately mausoleum stands there, in which a great emperor is sleeping peacefully. That is Fuling Imperial Tomb ("Fu" means blessings) of the founding father of Qing Dynasty, Nurhaci's tomb. Fuling Imperial Tomb is habitually called East Mausoleum by locals because it is located in the east of Shenyang.

Fuling Imperial Tomb lies on the bank of River Hun, with Mount Hui and Mount Tianzhu to its back, between which runs a Xinglong Ridge. However, as it goes, "no matter how high the mountain is, its name will spread far and wide if there is a 'mausoleum.'" Mount Tianzhu takes the advantage of Fuling Imperial Tomb and ranks one of the top scenic spots in Shenyang.

For me, Fuling Imperial Tomb has long been a place mixed with feelings of mystery and intimacy, where I have never had a chance to approach. At the age of twelve, I participated in the summer camp activities organized by Children's Palace. One of the arrangements that drove me excited was to pick Chinese hawthorn in Dongling Commune ("Dongling" means East Mausoleum). On our way there, we took a break on the square of front red gate of Mausoleum, which I had sketched with the rain water accumulated in motor tracks. I wondered what it would be like inside, but then only imagination could traverse beyond its red walls, because the doors were firmly locked. Mystery of the Mausoleum kept lingering in my mind and unrevealed.

At the age of 17, I covered a long way to Fuling Imperial Tomb with two of my friends, whom I made in Children's Palace with sketch boards. It took us half a day to take a bus, so I only finished a couple of sketches before it became dark. Before I went to college, I often went to the former Mausoleum fortress to draw sketches, but I never got an opportunity to go inside these red walls. When I was 19 years old, I should take the national university entrance exam. Grandma said to me that if I could be admitted, she would award me a camera. Although I failed that year, she still bought me a camera and encouraged me to try again. The next year, I was admitted to Luxun Fine Arts Institute as I had expected. Some of my father's students invited our family to go outing. They let me decide where to go as kind of reward. Without any hesitation, Dong Mausoleum jumped out of my mouth. It was the first time that I saw the panorama of Fuling Imperial Tomb, and I was then deeply shocked. That outing triggered my interest and led me to the threshold of ancient architecture. It paved the way for my study, research and protection of ancient buildings in my later life. From then on, I would like to go to Fuling Imperial Tomb to celebrate or relax myself by taking pictures there whenever I made some achievements or encountered certain hardships. The clicking of camera shutters would refresh my mind with compliments and encouragements. I have ever been enjoying no other exercises than shooting pictures, in which since then I have engaged myself quite often.

From the age of twelve on, I started to climb Mount Lv, Mount Tai, etc. After having visited all the well-known high mountains across China, I found that they are all higher than Mount Tianzhu in Shenyang, the summit of which is only above two hundred meters, even far behind the 1,000-meter-high Mount Qipan. Accordingly, I couldn't help thinking why Emperor Nurhaci chose Mount Tianzhu as his resting place. Pondering over the puzzle for many years, I learned later in my research that selecting mausoleum sites in ancient times follows the rule of "mirror in front and mountain behind," the standard of "geomancy," that is, facing water and resting upon mountains. A folk adage supports this idea as follows, "between two mountains runs a ridge and the line of empire will never ends." The site of Fuling Imperial Tomb matches the above standard perfectly, a hard-to-find invaluable land with a good geomantic omen. One law of geomancy is that mountains take form of dragons, and wherever there are mountains there is water. Therefore, "never find resting site in a mountain without water." In front of Fuling Imperial Tomb, there is a dragon beach, which is said to be the sand deposit of River Hui after years of accumulation. And this offsets the defect of water for the Mausoleum in terms of geomancy. Protected by Qing emperors, Mount Tianzhu has become a holy place in the hearts of Shenyang people. Its height is much higher than its actual elevation, because people lay more humanistic weights over its scientific concept, which is a kind of spirit, the spiritual pillar of Qing Dynasty. And I was trying to shoot down Mount Tianzhu, but couldn't find where the summit locates after walking around. Later, I found an earth slope from a point on the west side. I thought this might be Mount Tianzhu after thinking it over again and again because it is really only one or two hundred meters high. In the last three hundred years, the land has been well protected by the spontaneously organized locals. There are many descendants of the mausoleum defenders living in villages scattered about the former Mausoleum fortress areas, such as Zhao (肇), Zhao (赵), Na (那), He (贺), He (赫), Xi (西), who are Manchu people, but later many of whom have been assimilated by Han nationality.

Confucius once said: "the benevolent find joys in hills." (Note 1) In their selecting and planning of the mausoleum site, ancient Chinese were heavily influenced by the Confucian ideal "harmony between man and nature," which holds that man is endowed with the four cardinal virtues of human existence, i.e. humanity, justice, propriety and wisdom. In up to 27 characters of Nurhaci's posthumous name, there is a Chinese character "ren" (which means humanity), precisely reflecting the aspect that a true man loves the mountains. Humanity, which means being content with moral principles, manifests itself as tolerance, kindness, as firm and secure as mountains. The life of Nurhaci was full of battles and conquests. So many people can't help questioning that he was brutal and atrocious. Such arguments never ceased. There are many reasons why founding monarchs are cruel because they don't have a better alternative choice. Qin Shihuang, First Emperor of Qin Dynasty, burnt books and buried Confucian scholars alive, but after all, he was regarded as the first great Emperor; in his later years of Emperor Wudi in Han Dynasty, he killed many innocent people because of his deep belief in witchcraft, but he was appraised as a wise monarch. On the contrary, the humanity of Li Yu, Emperor in Late Tang Dynasty, led to the fall of an empire. However, the humanity of Nurhaci falls out of benevolence or kindness of a woman, but in the scope of righteousness. Guan Yu, Great General of Shu (蜀, a state of Zhou Dynasty) during Three Kingdoms Period, embodied with loyalty, humanity and braveness, is the hero most respected by Nurhaci. Many people want to be humane, but the truly humane people are rare, even fewer can become great righteous men. The humanity of Nurhaci is well interpreted by Fuling Imperial Tomb and its architecture. It is this imperial righteousness that attracts later generations to revere and worship, and this spiritual worship is ranked as high as heaven and as durable as mountains and rivers. To protect Fuling Imperial Tomb, we must protect the Mount, on which the Mausoleum perches on. The Mount is the integral part of Fuling Imperial Tomb, and also a part of the world cultural heritage.

With the deep silent spiritual faith in the interpretation of Fuling Imperial Tomb, there is a preference in my heart towards the Mausoleum. From the drawing at the beginning to the later concentration on shooting, I have been doing this job for at least 20 years. From 1998, every year I come here to take pictures, in which a lot of valuable information is kept, and the more valuable things are the memories associated with it. Many people say that the size and scale of Fuling Imperial Tomb is smaller than that of Zhaoling Imperial Tomb ("Zhao" means brightness). However, this does not affect the sacredness of Fuling Imperial Tomb in my heart. Three Mausoleums of Shengjing ("Shengjing" means a flourishing place in Manchu and refers to Shenyang today) include Yong Mausoleum ("Yong" means eternal), Fuling Imperial Tomb and Zhaoling Imperial Tomb. They have all been listed in World Heritage List of UNESCO, together with East and West Qing Mausoleums. These mausoleums compose the whole system of Qing emperors' mausoleums, condensing the history of Qing Dynasty, which are distinguished by various qualities and weights in my mind. As in the process of applying for World Cultural Heritage, they are a whole integrity which can not be viewed separately. We must study each of them with the consideration of the whole system. They are the unrepeated parts of the whole system, which also weigh differently in my heart.

There is probably a patch of woods, a pure piece of land in everyone's heart to rest his or her soul. Walking among the hundreds-years-old pines, enjoying the clear water, green trees and blue hills, calmness and delight spread in my heart.

At Shanwai Hall

福陵的爬山红墙／左页图
Uphill Red Wall of Fuling Imperial Tomb / Left Page

中国的陵寝学

研究中国古建筑，陵寝建筑是不可或缺的一部分。中国人对死很重视，古代一直尊崇"事死如生"的丧葬原则，《荀子·礼论》："丧礼者，以生者饰死者也，大象其生，以送其死，事死如生，事亡如存"。就是主张对待死者如他活着之时，从而形成了独具特色的中国陵寝学。在人分三六九等的古代社会，坟墓也有严格的等级区分。帝王的坟墓称为"陵"，圣人的坟墓称为"林"，王公贵族的坟墓称为"冢"，一般官员或富人的坟墓称为"墓"，平民百姓的坟墓则称为"坟"。而封建帝王从登基那天起最关注两件事，一是长生不老，二是修建自己的陵寝。因为古人认为，修建陵寝关系到江山社稷是否会万年永固。可以说中国的陵寝学，融合中国古代宗教学、风水学、建筑学、雕塑艺术、装饰艺术、绘画艺术等诸多文化艺术于一体。在建设陵寝过程中，以何种哲学思想为指导，是与当时的帝王的综合修养密切相关的。古代修建帝王陵寝，是国家的重要工程，在建设过程中，有多少人参与，发生了多少故事，以及在后世的祭祀与守护中，与朝代兴亡也有着密切的关系。

我为什么提出陵寝学这个概念，就是我从研究古建筑开始，就十分关注古代陵寝的建筑，尤其是帝王陵寝的建筑。在古代就算普通百姓安葬也讲究风水，何况是一代帝王。帝王陵寝建筑可以说是古建学中最高的学问，因为它并不是简单地涉及诸多的艺术门类，古代帝王都知道自己不可能长生不老，秦始皇十三岁登基，就开始为自己修陵。历代皇帝，都是一边让人喊万万岁，一边却早早就为自己大兴土木，建造地下宫殿，希望灵魂永生，精神不死。

这些年为了研究，我的足迹遍访祖国的名山大川，甚至漂洋过海，踏上异国他乡，只为寻找那些被时间的洪流淹没的历史的蛛丝马迹。回想一下，我到过的国内的陵寝有，人文初祖的黄帝陵、炎帝陵、大禹陵、少昊陵、秦始皇陵、汉武帝陵、光武帝陵，唐太宗陵、唐高宗和武则天陵、宋太祖赵匡胤、宋神宗赵顼、宋哲宗赵煦陵，元成吉思汗陵、明孝陵及十三陵（注解2）等；圣人墓，著名的山东曲阜的孔林，河南省洛阳市老城武圣关羽的关林和湖北当阳关林；先贤名人墓，有屈原墓、李白墓、杜甫墓、刘禹锡墓、岳飞墓、海瑞墓，还有喀什的香妃墓，这是我去过最西边的陵寝了。近代，更有人

宝顶神树 / 左图
Divine Tree on Blessed Vault / Left

尽皆知的中山陵。国外，有日本的奈良、京都的天皇陵寝、青山墓园、多摩墓园等。由于国家不同，文化也不同，西方国家的墓大都是公墓，像法国的先贤祠，是一个有强烈的宗教色彩的集体公墓。中国的陵寝学，可以说是世界之最，唯一可以与之媲美的，可能只有埃及的金字塔，只是两者也有极大的不同，中国的陵寝是纯粹为死者建造的，同时更注重风水以及福荫子孙后代。

从春秋时代，孔子大力提倡"孝道"开始，厚葬之风日盛，历代不衰，并逐渐形成一套隆重复杂的祭祀礼仪和墓葬制度。上至皇帝，下至百姓，对坟墓的安置均格外重视。我国古代帝王陵寝，从周代开始，以"封土为坟"，秦汉时期称为"方上"，汉朝以山为陵，就是在山里打个隧道，我认为这很了不起，中山靖王刘胜的墓以及双乳山汉墓都是如此。唐代则因山为陵，唐十八座皇陵中绝大多数都利用天然山丘，建在山岭顶峰处，居高临下，形成"南面为立，北面为朝"的形势。宋代帝陵则"头枕黄河，足蹬嵩岳"，乃"山高水来"的吉祥之地。宋陵在地形选择上与以往朝代不同，各陵皆东南高西北低。这是因为宋代盛行与汉代图宅术有关的"五音姓利"风水术，即把姓氏按五行分归五音，再按音选定吉利方位。赵，属于"角"音，利于壬丙方位，必须"东南地窊，西北地垂"。而明清以后则"宝城宝顶"，特别重视山川形胜，风水格外讲究，加之建筑的配合，皇陵的选择与规划都达到了空前的艺术水准。清朝陵寝的建造基本是沿袭明十三陵建造的，只是相比之下关内的清东陵与清西陵同明代陵寝风格上更相近，而清东陵这块风水宝地，曾被明朝皇帝派人选看过，只是后来改朝换代，才成为清帝陵了。关外三陵虽然也有明陵遗风，但却更具满族特色。至清代，中国的陵寝学，可以说是发展至巅峰。

福陵的方城、宝顶建筑在山顶上，这在其他历代帝王陵寝中是独一无二的。为什么把努尔哈赤的陵寝选在这里并建在山顶上呢？这就跟沈阳人口中时常念叨的"龙脉"（注解3）有关。提及龙脉，这就涉及风水学，风水学在古代又称为"堪舆学"，是相地之术，即临场校察地理的方法，目的是用来选择宫殿、城池、墓地建设等。风水学的历史相当久远，在古代，是衣食住行的一个很重要的因素。因此，许多与风水有关的知识和历史文献遗传和保留了下来。

MAUSOLEUM CULTURE IN CHINA

Mausoleum architecture is an integral part in the study of Chinese ancient architecture. Chinese people attach great importance to death and observe the funeral rule of "honoring the dead as the living." According to the principles of *On Rites in Book of Hsun Tzu*, "in the funeral rites, one uses objects of the living to adorn the dead and sends them to their grave in a fashion that resembles the way they lived. Thus one treats the dead like the living, and one treats their absence just as one treated them when they were still present." Such treatment of the dead as they were alive forms the unique funeral culture of China. People used to live in a society with strict and clear social status, and obviously hierarchy was also followed regarding funerals. For example, tomb of emperor was called "ling" (陵), and that of sage "lin" (林); tomb of nobility was named "zhong" (冢), that of common government official or rich people "mu" (墓), and that of civilians was "fen" (坟). From the day emperors were crowned, two things they most concerned about were how to be immortal and how to build their mausoleums, because in the eyes of ancient people, building of mausoleums counted for much because it might impact stability and rule of a dynasty. So the culture of mausoleum in China can be regarded as an integration of religion, fengshui (geomancy), architecture, sculpture, decorative arts, painting and many others. In the process of mausoleum construction, what philosophy would be employed was closely related to the comprehensive knowledge of an emperor. What's more, the building and construction of imperial mausoleums were highlighted as major national projects. Therefore in the process of construction, the number of people involved, the stories which had happened, and the sacrifice and mausoleum guarding of future generations are all closely related to the rise and fall of a dynasty.

The reason why the study of mausoleum culture as a science comes up in my mind is that as soon as I started the study of ancient architecture, I paid close attention to ancient tomb buildings, especially the imperial mausoleum architecture. Even ordinary people's burial in ancient also attached importance to geomancy, let alone the emperors'. Imperial mausoleum architecture can be considered as one of the most sophisticated branches of ancient architecture in a sense that it covers subjects of geomancy, architecture, religion, culture and arts. Emperors in ancient times knew that they could not be immortal. Qin Shihuang started the construction of his mausoleum after he crowned himself at the age of 13. The emperors in every dynasty on one hand enjoyed the longevity courtesy paid by their subjects, and on the other hand projected underground palaces for themselves as early as possible, hoping that their spirits could remain immortal.

In order to study ancient architecture, I visited many well-known historic relics and climbed many high mountains across China. I even went overseas to find those clues buried in the bed of the river of history. Tombs or mausoleums I visited include Huangdi Mausoleum (Huangdi, also Emperor Yellow, legendary ruler of ancient China), Yandi Mausoleum (Yandi, also Emperor Yan, another legendary ruler of ancient China), Dayu Mausoleum (Dayu, legendary first monarch of Xia Dynasty, best remembered for teaching the people flood-control techniques to tame China's rivers and lakes), Shaohao Tomb (Shaohao, son of Emperor Yellow and one of the mythical Five Emperors himself), Mausoleum of Qin Shihuang (first emperor of Qin Dynasty), Mausoleum of Emperor Wudi and Tomb of Emperor Guangwudi (of Han Dynasty), Mausoleums of Emperors Taizong, Gaozong and Wu Zetian (of Tang Dynasty), Mausoleums of Emperors Taizu (Zhao Kuangyin), Shenzong (Zhao Xu, 赵顼) and Zhezong (Zhao Xu, 赵煦) (of Song Dynasty), Genghis Khan's Mausoleum (of Yuan Dynasty), Xiao Mausoleum (for Hongwu Emperor, founder of Ming Dynasty) and Thirteen Tombs (of Ming

Dynasty) (Note 2). Other famous tombs are Confucius Family Graveyard in Qufu of Shandong Province, Guan Yu Graveyard in Luoyang of Henan Province (Guan Yu, a general serving under the warlord Liu Bei during the late Eastern Han Dynasty era of China) and Guan Yu Woods in Dangyang of Hubei Province (as head and body of Guan Yu were buried in different places). Tombs for wise men such as Qu Yuan, Li Bai, Du Fu, Liu Yuxi, Yue Fei, and Hai Rui are also my visiting destinations. Abakh Hoja Tomb in Kashgar, however, is the farthest that I visited in west China. Mausoleum of Dr. Sun Yatsen, a recent and well-known tomb, is of course included. I also paid visits to some famous overseas mausoleums such as mausoleums for Japanese emperors in Nara and Kyoto, Aoyama Cemetery, Tamareien Cemetery and so on. Despite their respective distinct cultural differences in different nations, cemeteries in Western countries are mostly public, such as Pantheon of France, which is typically an open graveyard with strong religious colors. Mausoleum culture in China has a long history and nothing but the pyramids of Egypt is on a par within this aspect. In contrast with pyramids, mausoleums in China were always constructed for the dead while emphasizing geomancy and blessings to their offspring of the tomb owners. And emperor mausoleums of Qing Dynasty are perfect examples to support my point of view.

From Spring and Autumn Period, Confucius advocated filial piety and the prevalence of lavish funeral practice spread and gradually a complex of rites and ceremonies and the burial system formed. Tomb arrangement and construction were paid great attention to by people from loyal families to ordinary households. From Zhou Dynasty, mausoleums in ancient China began to "bury the dead into grave mound." During Qin Dynasty, they were built with a "cubic shape on the ground." Han emperors took mountains as their last resting place, that is, they dug tunnels in mountains, which I think is unusual. Mausoleum of Liu Sheng, Prince Jin of Zhongshan, and Tomb of Mount Shuangru of Han Dynasty are of this type. Mountains were employed as emperors' mausoleums in Tang Dynasty, and most of their eighteen mausoleums take the advantages of mountains or hills. The mausoleums of Tang Dynasty, which were built on the topsides of natural mountains or hills, develop a political ideological pattern of "facing South to reign and facing North to obey," while the mausoleums of Song Dynasties, which rest emperors' heads upon River Huang and place their feet towards Mount Song, is considered as an auspicious place of "water from high mountain." The site selection of mausoleums of Song Dynasties are quite different from that of previous dynasties with the south-east part higher than that of the north-west. Because geomantic theory of "five notes and family name" was popular in Song dynasties, which is similar with the site selection of house and grave. The theory relates family names (classified into five elements) to five notes (of the ancient Chinese five-tone scale) and the bearing of house or grave is selected accordingly. According to this theory, the shared family name of Song Emperors is Zhao and it belongs to Jiao musical scale and the blessed place for Zhao is the east and the south. So, the principle of selecting mausoleum site "higher in the southeast and lower in the northwest" must be followed. During Ming and Qing dynasties, the mausoleums were built with "surrounded walls and domes," and elegant features of mountains and rivers are emphasized, and together with the matching architecture, the selection and planning of mausoleums reach an unprecedented level. Mausoleums of Qing Dynasty basically follow the construction of Ming Tombs only with East and East Qing Mausoleums inside Shanhai Pass sharing more similar features with mausoleums of Ming Dynasty. East Mausoleum sitting was once chosen by Ming Dynasty, but with the change of dynasties, it became the tomb site of Qing Dynasty. Three Mausoleums outside Shanhai Pass have some features of Ming mausoleums, but more Manchu characteristics. The culture of Chinese mausoleums and funerals reached to its heyday in Qing Dynasty.

The square city and dome of Fuling Imperial Tomb were built on the top of the hill. This is an exception among all mausoleums throughout all dynasties. Why did Nurhaci choose here and build his mausoleum on the top of the hill? It is related to the concept of "dragon vein" (Note 3), a popular idea held by Shenyang people. Dragon vein is related to geomancy, interpreting markings on the ground or the patterns of geographical features, which is used to select construction site of palace, city and cemetery. Geomancy boasts of a long history, which played an important role in every aspect in ancient time. So many historical literature and information related to geomancy are well preserved.

挂在大明楼上的福陵牌匾
Horizontal Board inscribed with "Fuling Imperial Tomb" on Grand Ming Tower

暮色隆恩门
Eminent Favor Gate at Dusk

为何定名为福陵？

福陵，满语称"瑚图灵阿蒙安"，创建于天聪三年（1629年），基本建成于清顺治八年（1651年），初称"太祖陵"、"先汗陵"。崇德元年（1636年）大清建国，定陵号为"福陵"，陵寝面积达19.48万平方米。《韩非子》曰"全寿富贵谓福"，取福气、运气之意，寓意大清福运长久。实际上当年的福陵是很简单的，只有山上几间房子，经康雍乾修葺和完善以后，才逐渐形成现在的规模的。福陵与新宾永陵、沈阳昭陵合称"关外三陵"或"盛京三陵"，三陵中福陵面积最大，永陵面积仅1.1万平方米，昭陵面积16万平方米。

《清太宗实录》（注解4）中记录了皇太极安奉乃父时的祭文，称福陵是"川萦山拱，佳气郁葱"，是极好的"万年吉地"。古代为皇帝选择的陵寝地址，一般称为"万年吉地"。顺治元年（1644年）钦定：修福陵于陵西五里外取土，西南二十里外烧砖，正南百里外烧石灰。《清实录》（注解5）顺治八年六月条载：以永陵为启运山，福陵为天柱山，昭陵为隆业山。天柱山，原名为"石嘴头山"，以"天柱"为陵山命名，寓意福陵犹如擎天大柱，支撑着大清江山。

福陵里面葬的是大清开国君主努尔哈赤及其孝慈高皇后叶赫那拉氏。陵寝建筑规制完备，礼制设施齐全，将中国古代环境地理学中宗教、信仰、习俗同自然环境相结合，使其达到建筑选址、规划、设计的统一，并成为中国古代陵寝建筑形式、雕刻以及综合理念的历史依据与鉴赏实物，对研究中国古代帝王陵寝建筑、规制及祭祀礼仪有着很重要的意义。所以2004年的时候，福陵就被列入了世界文化遗产名录。

WHY NAMED AS FULING IMPERIAL TOMB?

The building of Fuling Imperial Tomb was started in 1629 (the 3rd ruling year of Emperor Tiancong), and was completed in 1651 (the 8th year of Emperor Shunzhi's reign). Fuling Imperial Tomb was then called "Taizu Mausoleum" or "Forefather Khan's Mausoleum." In 1636 (the first ruling year of Emperor Chongde), the founding year of Imperial Qing Dynasty, the mausoleum was renamed as Fuling Imperial Tomb with coverage of 194,800 square meters. According to *Book of Han Feizi*, "Ripe age and richness are Fu," a connotation of good fortune and luck, which implies wishes of long lasting reign of Qing Dynasty. Originally, Fuling Imperial Tomb consisted of only a few simple houses on the hill after it was built. It reaches the current scale only after renovation and additional construction were made by later emperors. Fuling Imperial Tomb, Zhaoling Imperial Tomb in Shenyang and Yong Mausoleum in Xinbin County are called "Three Mausoleums of Shengjing" or "Three Mausoleums outside the Pass." Of the three mausoleums, Fuling Imperial Tomb covers the largest area, Yong Mausoleum covers 11,000 square meters and Zhaoling Imperial Tomb covers 160,000 square meters.

The funeral oration recorded in Chronicles of Hong Taiji (Note 4) thinks highly of Fuling Imperial Tomb as "winding river and green mountains holding the blessing," which is an "auspicious land." In ancient China, mausoleum site selected by emperors is generally called "auspicious land." In 1644, the first ruling year of Emperor Shunzhi, he gave imperial edict as follows: To renovate Fuling Imperial Tomb, earth is excavated five li away to the west of Mausoleum, brick made twenty li away to the southwest and lime kilned hundred li away to the south. According to Records of Qing Dynasty (Note 5), one of the records of June in the 8th ruling year of Emperor Shunzhi reads as: "To keep Yong Mausoleum as Mount Qiyun (which means provoking luck), Fuling Imperial Tomb as Mount Tianzhu (which means supproting pillar), and Zhaoling Imperial Tomb as Mount Longye (which means prosperity and wealth)." Mount Tianzhu, formerly known as "Mount Shuzuitou," adopts the name of "Tianzhu" indicating the supporting pillar, which supports Great Qing Dynasty.

Inside Fuling Imperial Tomb, Nurhaci and his queen, Xiaocigao (Yehe Nara Menggu) were buried. Together with its complete set of mausoleum standards and ritual facilities, Fuling Imperial Tomb integrates religion, beliefs and customs of ancient Chinese environmental geography with nature. and unifies its building site selection, planning and design, which succeeds in transforming the architectural and sculptural concepts of ancient Chinese mausoleum architecture into physical forms, and attaches important significance to the study of Chinese ancient imperial mausoleum construction, standards, and etiquettes of sacrifice. So in 2004, Fuling Imperial Tomb was recorded onto List of World Cultural Heritage.

官员至此下马

福陵从建陵开始，300年间成为皇家禁地，当年这里设有"青、白、红三色界桩"，不许百姓涉足。《大清律》规定："红桩以内寸草为重，白桩以内禁止采樵，青桩以内禁止烧造"。擅自进入陵区，杖刑一百。如果是守陵官兵有意将其放入，要受同样刑罚。进入陵区打柴、牧放牲畜者要杖刑八十，对打猎惩罚更严重，除受杖刑之外，还要枷号两个月或发配充军。不仅如此，陵前三面还有"栅木"（挡众木）1514架，这些既是陵界标志也是安全防护设施，守陵人也由最初的12人发展到进关后的总管衙门和掌官防两衙门执行管理，形成了一套专门的管理机构。威严的律法，醒目的界桩，再加上在风水墙外昼夜巡视的八旗官兵，游览皇陵，老百姓是想都不敢想的。

如今，福陵的那些界桩都随着清朝的覆灭而消失了，只剩下马碑，两座立在正红门道前，距离约170米。两座在东西红门附近，碑文都为满、蒙、汉三种语言写着："官员人等至此下马"。我一直在想，官员人等下马，那究竟包不包括皇帝呢？按官职说，皇帝是无品级的，百官都是皇帝封的，从历史的角度看，皇帝又可以说是古代最高级别的官了。而中国的皇帝一向是以孝治天下的，是天下忠孝的楷模，坐轿进祖宗陵寝显然又是说不通的。有一种说法是，皇帝祭祀的时候从东红门进入陵寝，我认为这种说法并不合理。假设如此，君门这种象征级别的建筑岂不成了空设？类推到供皇帝使用的御厕、更衣厅岂不也都成了虚设。东红门下马碑没有正对着东红门，至东红门距离约88米，与风水红墙的垂直距离约31米。西红门下马碑与西红门正对，而碑至西红门距离约91米。东红门外是深沟险壑，西红门外是密林小道，两处都很难行走，可以说这两处下马碑只是象征性的建筑，并没有实际意义。和昭陵下马碑相比，福陵下马碑离陵寝距离更近，因为福陵整体规制也相对较小。

据我研究，这些石碑立于两个时期。乾隆四十四年（1779年）之前有石下马碑和木下马牌两种标志。乾隆四十八年，皇帝东巡才将木牌改为石碑。根据《黑图档》（注解6）等资料记载，乾隆连续从夏园和盛京两次传旨，将"盛京永陵、福陵、昭陵并宫殿东西鹿角外旁所有原设木下马碑，均改换石下马碑。镌刻满、蒙、藏、维、汉五种字以昭我国家一统，同文之盛。"因此，原来的木下马碑就换成了石下马碑。

清朝陵寝的建造基本是沿袭明十三陵建造，而加以改进的，下马碑的使用也是由明陵而来，关外三陵都设有下马碑。永陵里有两座下马碑，昭陵里有六座。令我不解的是，为什么昭陵里下马碑有五种文字和三种文字，而福陵里现存的只有三种文字，当年乾隆帝明明要求三陵都换石下马碑，难道在古代也有"上令下不行"的时候？我一直试图寻找福陵全部的下马碑，找了二十年，西侧的一个已无踪影，东侧的在红墙内东南角处寻到，不知何时何人将碑迁移至此。

碑的使用要追溯到东汉以前，古人

把长方形的刻石叫碑，把圜首形的或形在方圆之间的叫碣。东汉以来，碑碣渐多，有碑颂、碑记，又有墓碑，用以记事颂德，碑的形式也有了一定的要求。有资料记载，秦始皇曾在公元前219年率众臣登泰山封禅，并在泰山顶的碧霞祠西侧玉女池畔立碑歌功颂德，以诏天下。颂文由当时的丞相、书法家李斯以小篆撰写，此碑直至宋代才消失，可能是时间太久而风化，据说清乾隆时发现了碑文的残片，保留至今。曹操最著名的诗句"东临碣石，以观沧海"，虽然这里的碣石是山名，但足以说明，碣在当时已经存在。到了清朝时，一般颂扬人、物等的政府文告为长期传播，就经常刻成石碑立于村头镇尾，如现存四川"禁杀耕牛"就是很好的碑证。在中国古代，碑碣就是广告。而清朝的下马碑，用现代语言讲就是交通禁止。福陵和昭陵的下马碑相比，福陵的碑在山上，离门很近；而昭陵的碑在平地上，离门远。

如今这些下马碑，在现代人眼里已经失去了其作用，只是徒留一丝庄严与敬畏在心中吧。福陵，早在1929年就被奉天政府开辟成公园，因此很多人都能够进去看看。我想，当初的皇家禁地，如今平常老百姓也可以进，这是社会的一种进步，只是也难免感慨，世事沧桑难料，努尔哈赤怎么也不会想到自己的陵寝会成为百姓的游园吧，如此一来，这里的文物保护工作也更加艰巨了。

OFFICIALS DISMOUNT HERE

In the last 300 years, i.e. from the building of Fuling Imperial Tomb, it became the imperial forbidden area with blue, white and red pillars to warn ordinary people to keep away from here. Laws of Great Qing stipulates, "everything should be protected within red pillars; no firewood can be gathered within white pillars; no burning or farming is permitted within blue pillars." Unauthorized access to Mausoleum area would result in one hundred strokes of stick punishment. Mausoleum protection solders who let people in without authorization will receive the same punishment. Gathering firewood and herding livestock would result in eighty strokes of stick punishment. Hunting in Mausoleum area would face more serious punishment, in addition to stick punishment; he would be put into jail with cangue on his neck for two months or exiled to serve in the army. What's more, there are one thousand five hundred and fourteen sets of palisade (blocking wood) in three directions, which are both boundary markers of Mausoleum and safety facilities. The Mausoleum protection organization of 12 people developed into two specialized management agencies i.e. Imperial Household Bureau and Bureaucratic Management Department. Strict laws and striking boundary pillars, together with Eight Banners patrol soldiers outside the geomantic walls day and night, make it impossible for ordinary people to visit imperial Mausoleum.

Today, those boundary pillars of Fuling Imperial Tomb have already disappeared with the fall of Qing Dynasty. Only five dismounting tablets are left, about 170 meters away. There are two dismount tablets at west and east red gates. On tablets, there are auspicious patterns and inscriptions of "Everyone ranked below chieftain shall dismount" engraved in five languages, i.e. Chinese, Hui, Tibetan, Mongolian and Manchu. I keep thinking whether the emperor is included in the above mentioned "officers." According to the official ranks, the emperor is rank-free and he appoints all the officials; but from the perspective of history, we believe that the emperor is the highest rank of official in ancient times. If an emperor does not dismount here, where does he dismount? By reason, he shall dismount here, too; because it shows lack of respect to his ancestors to sit in a sedan into the ancestral tomb. Emperors in ancient China have always been ruling the country based upon filial piety, and they are the models of loyalty and filial piety for the whole world; he values rites more than anyone else when he enters the ancestral tomb, except due to old age or illness. It is also said that an emperor does not go by the front red gate but the east red one; in that case, will the building that is symbolic for monarchial power become just nominal? Not only the front red gate, but others such as royal toilet and dressing room all become nominal.

The dismounting tablets at east red gate don't face East Red Gate. They are about 88 meters away from East Red Gate and 31 meters to geomantic red wall. The dismounting tablets at west red gate are 91 meters away from West Red Gate. The dismounting tablets at East Red Gate and West Red Gate have no practical meaning, because there is a big ditch outside East Red Gate and a narrow path outside West Red Gate. Dismounting tablets then are only symbolic buildings. Compared with dismounting tablets in Zhaoling Imperial Tomb, its distance between dismounting tablets and Mausoleum is much shorter, because the scale of Fuling Imperial Tomb is smaller than that of Zhaoling Imperial Tomb.

According to my study, these tablets were erected in two periods. Before the 44th ruling year of Emperor Qianlong (1779), there were two types of dismounting tablets: stone and wooden. In the 48th ruling year of Emperor Qianlong, the wooden ones were changed into stone ones during his tour to the East. According to Heitu Records (Note 6) and other resources, Emperor Qianlong gave two imperial edicts from Xia Garden and Shengjing to "change all the wooden dismounting tablets of Yong Mausoleum, Fuling Imperial Tomb, Zhaoling Imperial Tomb and other palaces into stone dismounting tablets, and engrave five languages of Manchu, Chinese, Mongolian, Tibetan and Hui nationality to show unification and prosperity of the empire." Therefore, the original wooden tablets were changed to stone ones.

Mausoleums of Qing Dynasty basically follow the construction of Thirteen Tombs of Ming Dynasty with some improvements. The use of dismounting tablets came from tradition of Ming Tombs. All the three Mausoleums adopted dismounting tablets. There are two dismounting tablets in Yong Mausoleum and six in Zhaoling Imperial Tomb. I am puzzled as to why there are the dismounting tablets with five languages or

五种字体下马碑（官员人等至此下马）／左页图
Dismounting Tablets with Inscriptions of Five Languages (Officials of any Rank and Common People Dismount Here and Common People Dismount Here) / Left Page
[碑为褐色砂石，宽1.11米，厚0.45米，碑头刻有如意形纹]
(The tablet is made of brown sand stone, 1.11 meters wide and 0.45 meter thick, with auspicious patterns inscribed on its tablet head)

西下马碑／左页图
West Dismounting Tablet / Left Page
东下马碑／上图
East Dismounting Tablet / Upper
[碑宽 1.1 米，厚 0.45 米，高 4.3 米，座高 0.9 米。]
(The tablet is 1.1 meters wide, 0.45 meter thick and 4.3 meters high, with its base 0.9 meter high)

three languages in Zhaoling Imperial Tomb while there are only dismounting tablets with three languages present in Fuling Imperial Tomb. Emperor Qianlong obviously required changing old dismounting tablets with stone ones. Is it possible that the officials who carried out this order disobeyed? In the past twenty years, I have been trying to find all the dismounting tablets in Fuling Imperial Tomb, but there is not any trace of them in the west side. However, the tablets in the east side are found inside Red Walls, and I have no idea about when the tablets were moved here and who did this.

The use of tablets can be dated back to Eastern Han Dynasty. Stone tablets in ancient times could be divided into two categories, Bei (碑), rectangular shaped, and Jie (碣), dome shaped on top. From Eastern Han Dynasty, stone tablets became popular and were used to record or praise in forms of panegyric tablets, event record tablets and gravestones. It is recorded that Qin Shihuang went to Mount Tai to offer sacrifices to Heaven with his court in 219 B.C. A stone tablet was erected beside Yunv Pool, to the west of Bixia Temple, to honor virtues and achievements of Qin Dynasty. The panegyric was drafted by the grand councilor and calligrapher, Li Si. The tablet disappeared in Song Dynasty, possibly because of long time wear-out of weather. It is said some fragments were found during the reign of Emperor Qianlong and had been preserved. In the most famous poem of Cao Cao, "Standing atop the Rocky Hill, I gaze out at the wide East Sea," a word Jie (碣) is used in the poem. Although the word used in the poem doesn't mean the tablet, we still can infer that the word existed at that time. In Qing Dynasty, the general official notices for long-term spreading, or praising people and recording events, etc. were often carved onto stone, which stood on the side of road for publicity. "No farming cattle can be slaughtered" found in Sichuan is a good example of this kind. In an era without paper, steles were used as advertising media. Interpreted in modern language, dismounting tablet in Qing Dynasty is a traffic warning. Comparatively speaking, the distance between dismounting tablets and the gate of Fuling Imperial Tomb are much nearer than that of Zhaoling Imperial Tomb, because these dismounting tablets are located in the hill, while the dismounting tablets of Zhaoling Imperial Tomb are further away from the gate, because they are located on the ground.

Today, these dismounting tablets are losing their original functions, with only a trace of solemnity and awe left behind in people's heart. As early as 1929, Fuling Imperial Tomb was transformed into a park by Mukden Government, so many people were able to go inside and have a close look at it. The past royal forbidden area is now accessible to ordinary people, which I think is the demonstration of social progress. But inevitably one can't help thinking of the unpredictable vicissitudes of life because Nurhaci never thought that his tomb would be a garden for people to visit. And the work of heritage preservation and protection will be more difficult than ever.

失去下马功能的牌坊

福陵,正红门东西两侧,各有一座石造牌楼,两牌楼之间距离约130米,历史远去,两座牌楼却依然矗立在街上,提示着人们,这里曾经壁垒森严。福陵的两个牌坊是石头的,这样的牌坊在昭陵正红门正中也有一个,而沈阳故宫东西两牌坊却是木制的。因为各自修建的年代不一样,所以选用的材料也不一样。牌楼,起源于棂星门(注解7),开始用于祭天、祀孔,滥觞于汉阙,成熟于唐、宋,至明、清登峰造极。牌楼,实际上是起一个门的作用,只是它的建筑形式是用牌坊。牌坊的原始雏形名为"衡门",是由两根柱子架一根横梁构成的最简单、最原始的门。最早的记载见于《诗·陈风·衡门》:"衡门之下,可以栖迟。"据此推断,衡门最迟在春秋中叶就已经出现,后来被运用到城市居民区间的"坊门"上。从春秋战国至唐代,我国城市居民区都采用里坊制,"坊"与"坊"之间有墙相隔,坊墙中央设坊门,逐渐演变成后来的牌坊。通常情况下,牌楼、牌坊的称呼相互通用,但其实坊和楼还有些微小的区别。

牌坊,从用途上可分为四种,分别是功德牌坊、贞洁道德牌坊、家族牌坊、标志牌坊。从形式上分,只有两类,一类叫"冲天式",也叫"柱出头"式,另一类"不出头"式。造型上均有"一间二柱"、"三间四柱"、"五间六柱"等,顶上楼数,则有"一楼、三楼、五楼、七楼、九楼"等。无论哪种形式树牌坊都是旌表德行,承沐后恩,流芳百世之举,也是古人一生境界的最高追求,因为牌坊是不能随意建的,必须有皇帝的批准才能建。在古代,为了表彰一个人的事迹,给他立个牌坊,可以说是最高荣誉了。和碑碣一样,这也是最早的一种广告形式。今天,在皖南徽州地区,牌坊与民居、祠堂并列被称为"古建三绝",徽州牌坊原有一千多个,现仍存百余个,被誉为"牌坊之乡"。而山东西南的单县,因"百寿坊"、"百狮坊",也有"牌坊县"之称。这些牌坊,都成了永恒的"忠贞、节烈"的广告宣传形式。

陵寝建筑里的牌坊和市井建筑牌坊,在功能上略有不同,它是祭礼仪注的起点,就是说祭陵人进入牌坊就进入祭祀状态,应注重仪礼了。此外,也起到装饰陵寝、增加气势的作用。清福陵里这对石牌坊又叫下马石牌坊,和下马碑有着同样功能,同时也是福陵中最早的建筑物。《清太宗实录》上记载,天聪三年"陵东、西两旁立下马坊,禁乘车马行走,遇必下,诸贝勒大臣以下,小民以上。违者罚。"坊上的文字"往来人等至此下马如违定依法处"与《实录》这条记载相符合。因为后来乾隆修陵的时候在牌坊的东西又立了下马碑,就下马牌坊与下马碑之间的距离而言,也仅百米而已。西侧整一百米,比东侧距离稍微远些,东侧则约95米,由此我想,可能古人丈量得也不一定精确,也会有误差。福陵立碑后下马的距离离福陵更远了,三陵中,永陵没有牌坊,而与昭陵相比,福陵修建得比较早,昭陵修建得晚。昭陵下马碑规定中分了两个级别,"诸王以下"和"官员人等",而福陵中还没有这个分别。即使今天看来,福陵中的牌坊也完全失去了下马的功能,因为改路以后,西侧下马坊后的路上被种上了树,基本无路,而东侧也只是仅存一段小路,时至今日,下马牌坊只起装饰和纪念作用了。

皇太极为其父亲修建的福陵,历经几代人的修葺与完善,才逐渐建成。对两陵的认识,可以说是对整个大清王朝从开始到鼎盛的认识,也是整个大清王朝的历史缩影。因为清朝统治中国时间长达近三百年,所以,陵寝从建造开始,必然要经历破损和后世维修,这样,里面的很多建筑年代不一,甚至同一建筑的不同部分年代也不一。

福陵的牌坊,在嘉庆十年(公元1805年)嘉庆帝要东巡祭祖时,做过一次大修。因为福陵里东侧下马坊的地脚发生沉陷,坊身倾斜,同年三月盛京又刮了一场暴风,将已倾斜的牌坊上半部分吹落了,牌坊断成两截。要在皇帝祭祖前短短几个月时间,重新建造一座石牌坊是根本不可能的。盛京工部官员想出一个先用木料代替石料,在石座上安装半截木牌楼,待皇帝东巡结束后重新复原的办法。嘉庆东巡之后,石牌坊才恢复原貌。同样,昭陵里的牌坊,也在嘉庆六年做过重修,当时的牌坊,仅在两端有三对夹杆石兽(狮子二对,獬豸一对),而中间立柱前后的两对夹杆石兽则建造于嘉庆六年。仔细看,就会看出中间两对石狮颜色较白,而两端的石兽颜色较深。

福陵里的石牌坊,四柱三间三楼。全长10.50米,宽3.13米,基座高1.66米,宽1.1米,基座前后各有抱鼓石,鼓心是莲花形,下面雕有锦袱,锦袱两角各坠古钱一枚。抱鼓石下是须弥座,岔角石上刻有缠枝纹,每根石柱由四节组成,立柱顶端有一圆形的莲花座,上面各有一只望天吼。楼为歇山式,斗栱、滴水、勾头、大脊等构件俱全。坊额里面雕刻有仙人献宝、松、柏、祥云、海水、喜鹊等图案,南间坊心其外面雕有鲤鱼跳龙门,仙人击鼓;里面雕有海水江涯、仙人童子。北间坊心刻有仙人骑兽、神鸟、海水江涯,外面雕有仙人、蟒蛇、祥云。整个牌坊的雕工古朴、典雅、十分精美。严格地讲,这里的牌坊,其实是牌楼(注解8),因为它有顶,

西石牌坊/右图
West Stone Paifang / Right

而顶是等级的一个象征。从这里也可以看出，福陵牌坊是清朝刚建国的时候立的，就地取材，石质比较粗糙，上面有黑色蜂眼儿。昭陵的石材则是从山海关外运来的，石料上等，石质细腻。

PAIFANG: LOSING THE FUNCTION OF DISMOUNTING

On either side of front red gate of Fuling Imperial Tomb, there is a stone pailou, a decorated gateway or arch. The distance between these two pailous is about 130 meters. The two arches are still standing in the street, suggesting that it was once a closely guarded imperial garden. The two pailous at Fuling Imperial Tomb are made of stone, the same as the one located at the front red gate of Zhaoling Imperial Tomb. However, the two paifangs on the east and west sides of Shenyang Imperial Palace are wooden ones. Because pailous are built in different eras, the materials used differ. Pailous originated from Lingxing Gate (Note 7), which was first used to offer a sacrifice to Heaven and worship Confucius. They derived from watchtowers of Han Dynasty, developed in Tang and Song Dynasties, and reached the peak of perfection in Ming and Qing Dynasties. Pailous in fact function as gates. However, they take the form of paifangs. Original name of paifangs is called "beam door," with a beam laid on the tops of two pillars, which is the simplest and most primitive form of the door. Beam door was first recorded in the poem "Beam Door" of "Songs from Chen" in *The Book of Poetry*, "Under a beam door, one can enjoy leisure." We can infer that beam door appeared no later than the middle of Spring and Autumn Period. Beam door was later applied to district street gates in urban areas. From Spring and Autumn Period and Warring States Period to Tang Dynasty, China's urban areas adopted Lifang system, i.e. district block system. Walls were built between different district blocks and in the middle of these walls gates were erected, which gradually evolved into paifangs and pailous later. There are slight differences between paifangs and pailous.

Paifangs fall into four categories in terms of function: Merit & Virtue Paifang, Chastity Paifang, Family Paifang, and Identity Paifang. In terms of form, there are only two categories, one called "sky-pointing style," or "protruding type," and the other "non-protruding type." Modeling of paifangs could be "1 bay 2 pillars," "3 bays 4 pillars" and "5 bays 6 pillars," and the number of cockloft could be one, three, five, seven, nine, etc. Whatever form of paifangs people erected, they hoped to honor the virtues and deeds, bring blessings to offspring, or leave a good name behind, which reflected the summit pursuit of ancient Chinese. But paifangs couldn't be built at will unless it was approved by the emperor's edict. In ancient times, it was the highest honor to build a paifang for a person in recognition of his or her deeds or virtues. Like stone tablets, this is one of the earliest forms of advertising. Today, in Huizhou of southern Anhui Province, paifangs, houses of locals and their ancestral temples are called "Three Pearls of Ancient Architecture." There used to be more than a thousand paifangs in Huizhou, and now there are still more than one hundred left, thus Huizhou is named as the "Hometown of Paifang." Shanxian County, in the southwest of Shandong Province, famous for paifangs of "Bai Shou Fang" and "Bai Shi Fang," is also wellknown as "County of Paifangs." These paifangs have become everlasting advertising forms of fidelity and chastity.

Paifangs of mausoleum architecture and those of urban area are of little difference in terms of function in that it is the starting point of sacrificial rites, that is, people who offer sacrifice to mausoleums must come to a state of worshiping with attention concentrated on the ceremony. What's more, paifangs play roles of adding ornaments and imposing grandeur to mausoleums. The couple of stone paifangs in Fuling Imperial Tomb are also called dismounting stone paifangs, having the same function of dismounting tablets, and they are also the oldest buildings in Fuling Imperial Tomb. According to Chronicles of Hong Taiji, in the third ruling year of Tiancong, ".... dismounting paifangs are built on the east and west sides of Fuling Imperial Tomb, all officials under the rank of Baylors and common people shall dismount to show courtesy. Any violation leads to severe punishment." The inscription on paifangs coincides with the records above. During the renovation by Emperor Qianlong, two dismounting tablets were established on the west and east sides of paifangs. The distance between west

东石牌坊／左页图
East Stone Paifang / Left Page
[长10.36米，宽2.73米，高8.7米]
(10.36 meters long, 2.73 meters wide, 8.7 meters high)
西石牌坊"往来人等至此下马，如违定依法处"铭文／下图
Inscriptions on West Stone Paifang, "Officials under Rank of Royal Highness and Common People Dismount Here, and Any Violation Leads to Severe Punishment" / Lower

dismounting tablet and paifang is 100 meters, a little further than that between east dismounting tablet and paifang, which is about 95 meters. I think that the measurement in ancient times might not be so accurate. I'm wondering whether Emperor Qianlong knew this. Since the erection of dismounting tablets, the distance between dismounting point and Fuling Imperial Tomb became even farther. Of the three mausoleums, there is no dismounting tablet in Yong Mausoleum; the building of Fuling Imperial Tomb was earlier than Zhaoling Imperial Tomb. In Zhaoling Imperial Tomb, the people who need to dismount were divided into two categories: "ranks below chieftains" and "officials and ordinary people," but there is no such distinction in Fuling Imperial Tomb. Even viewed from today, paifangs in Fuling Imperial Tomb had totally lost its dismounting function, as the road behind the western dismounting tablet was covered with trees, and the road in the eastern side was left almost no space. Dismounting Paifangs can only serve as decoration and commemoration.

Fuling Imperial Tomb, built by Hong Taiji for his father, gradually develops into its current scale after several generations of renovation and improvement. Understanding of these two Mausoleums, the miniature of the history of Qing Dynasty, is the key to understanding how Qing Dynasty rose to its peak. The reign of Qing Dynasty lasted in China for nearly three hundred years, which means that these Mausoleums, from their beginning of construction, were bound to experience damage and renovation in future. So there are many buildings built in different times with different styles. Even on the same building, different parts demonstrate much renovation and repair done in different times.

Paifangs of Fuling Imperial Tomb experienced major repairs in the 10th ruling year of Emperor Jiaqing (1805) when he paid respects and offered sacrifices to his ancestors during his tour to the East. The ground in the east side of Fuling Imperial Tomb sank and the body of paifang tilted. What's more, a storm stroke Shengjing in March the same year and blew off the upper part of paifang, which was smashed into two sections. It was simply impossible to rebuild a stone paifang in a few months before Emperor came to pay his respects to his ancestors. An official of Ministry of Works in Shengjing came up with an idea that a wooden pailou could be built on the stone seat and it could be replaced after Emperor's worship to his ancestors. After Jiaqing's tour, the wooden pailou was restored to its original. Similarly, paifang in Zhaoling Imperial Tomb, built in years of Shunzhi, also experienced renovation in the 6th ruling year of Emperor Jiaqing. There were only three pairs of stone pillars supporting animals at the outer pillars of the paifang (two pairs of lions and a pair of justice animals), while the stone pillar supporting animals in middle were built in the 6th year of Emperor Jiaqing. If you have a close look at them, you will find that the two pairs of stone animals in the middle are a little whiter, while the stone animals at the outer pillars are darker in color.

The stone paifangs in Fuling Imperial Tomb are 4 pillars, 3 bays and 4 cocklofts. Measurements of the paifang are 10.5 meters long, 3.13 meters wide and those of its base stone are 1.66 meters high, 1.1 meters wide. There are drum-shaped bearing stones in both the front and the back of base stone. The drum center is lotus-shaped, and a colorful scarf is engraved below lotus with two coins hanging on two corners of the scarf. Under the drum-shaped bearing stone there is Sumeru throne. Winding pattern lines are engraved on interlocking corner stone. Each pillar is composed of four sections, on top of which lies a round lotus-like base, with a Sky Roaring Hou (one of nine sons of dragon) sitting on it. Hip and gable roofs are used for cocklofts, which are full of bracket sets, drip tiles, eave tiles, main beam and other components. In the center of paifang, inscriptions of three languages are engraved on it with Manchu on the left, Mongolian on the right and Chinese at center. Chinese reads as "Officials and ordinary people dismount here. Any violation will result in severe punishment according to the law," which creates a majestic and stern atmosphere. Patterns and drawings of treasure presenting, pines, cypresses, auspicious cloud, sea water, magpies and others are engraved on paifang tablets. On the outside center of southern paifang, Carps Jumping over Dragon Gate and Drum Beating by Immortal are engraved; inside inscribes auspicious tiding lines and treasure stones and celestial beings and fairy boys. In the north center of paifang, there are riding animals of immortals, fairy birds, auspicious tiding lines and treasure stones. Outside inscribes celestial beings, dragonet and auspicious cloud. Overall sculpture of the paifang is simple, elegant, delicate and beautiful. Strictly speaking, paifangs of Fuling Imperial Tomb are pailous (Note 8), because there are tops on them, which is the symbol of hierarchy. But from this it can also be seen that paifangs of Fuling Imperial Tomb were built just after the founding of Qing Dynasty. The building materials are from nearby, because the stones are rough ones with black holes in them. In contrast, the stones of Zhaoling Imperial Tomb were shipped from Hebei Province with high quality and fine texture.

西石牌坊的抱鼓石 / 右页图
Drum-shaped Bearing Stone of West Stone Paifang / Right Page

正红门／左图、上图
Front Red Gate / Left, Upper
[长15.93米，宽9.91米，高9.76米，共三间，拱形洞门，每间内宽2.10米，高2.80米]
(The Gate is 15.93 meters long, 9.91 meters wide and 9.76 meters high. There are 3 rooms inside with each 2.1 meters wide and 2.8 meters high, and its doorways all in arch form)

正红门的学问

福陵陵寝的正门是大红门，又叫正红门，它有三个门洞。许多人认为中间的门是给皇帝走的，其实皇帝当年走的是东侧门洞。正红门，单檐歇山式仿木架结构，砖石垒砌，油灰灌浆，非常坚固。上顶满铺琉璃瓦，下有台基。正红门前后门橡镶有半圆形石"券脸"，明间券脸上雕二龙戏珠，左右次间雕有云纹。门下部有高70厘米的石台基，台基与昭陵不同，福陵红门就在广场上，没有落差，且无护栏、栏板及望柱，台基前后各有三路台阶。正红门，有拱门三道，彩油为饰，门上兽面"铺首"。作一个简单的比较，福陵正红门没有门钉，永陵没有正红门，只有一道栅栏门，且无门钉，而昭陵正红门，在第二层的台阶上，且门扇两面都有门钉。关内清陵正红门与关外清陵的正红门也有很大不同，有的甚至没有红门与红墙，如道光帝的慕陵和慈禧的定东陵，是灰黄色墙，这也是清朝皇家谦虚罪己的一种方式。有的，则没有琉璃袖壁，如顺治帝的孝陵。

福陵正红门可谓等级森严，智慧无所不在，所在之处又无所不用其极。就连简单的一道门，也是深藏玄机。三门中，正中一间叫"神门"，是供墓主"神灵"出入的，平日不开，只有在大祭时供抬祝版、制帛等祭品的官员出入。古人对此门很敬畏，也很忌讳。比如皇帝、皇后以及王公大臣如需从门前经过，必须事先在门前用芦席搭盖帷幕遮挡，甚至不敢向内窥视；东次间叫"君门"，是皇帝祭陵出入的；西次间叫"臣门"，是祭祀大臣走的。《大清世祖实录》明确规定："祭福陵、昭陵，上（皇帝）躬往，自左门（东次间）入，若遣官，自右门（西次间）入，祭文、祭品悉由中门入。"然而在具体实施时也可以有所"变通"。

正红门外东侧石狮／左页图
East-side Stone Lion outside Front Red Gate / Left Page
臣门、神门、君门竖腰石石刻／上图
Inscriptions on Vertical Waist Stones for Door of Officials,
Door of Spirit and Door of Emperor/Upper

ENIGMA OF FRONT RED GATE

The main entrance of Fuling Imperial Tomb is Great Red Gate, also called Front Red Gate, a three gateway structure. Many people think that the middle one is for emperors, but in fact, the east gateway we take now is the one that emperors took at that time. The Gate is of a stone and brick masonry with putty grouting, which has a structure of single hip and gable roof, imitating wooden structure, and is therefore firm, stable and delicate. The roof is covered with glazed tiles, under which there is a platform. On the front and back parts of gate frame of Front Red Gate, there are semi-circle face stones. There are patterns of Two Dragons Playing with a Pearl engraved on the main frame and cloud patterns on both sides of frames. Under the gate there is a 0.7-meter-high stone base, which is different from that of Zhaoling Imperial Tomb. The red gate of Fuling Imperial Tomb is located on the square, so there is no drop in elevation. There are only three flights of stairs side by side in the front and at the back of the base, without rails, guard plates or balusters on it. Front Red Gate consists of three arches, decorated with colored paint, with golden nails on doors and animal head appliqué of "Pu Shou".

To make a simple comparison, there is no doornail on Front Red Gate of Fuling Imperial Tomb; there is no Front Red Gate but only a fence with no doornail in Yong Mausoleum, while there are doornails on both sides of Front Red Gate, which is fixed on the second storey of the platform in Zhaoling Imperial Tomb. Great differences lie between Front Red Gates of the mausoleums inside and outside Shanhai Pass. Some of the mausoleums even don't have any red gates or red walls. For example, the walls of Emperor Daoguang's Mu Mausoleum and Cixi's East Ding Mausoleum are greyish yellow, which is a way to show their modest and humble attitude of Qing royal family. And some mausoleums don't even have glazed screen walls, for example, Emperor Shunzhi's Xiao Mausoleum.

Front Red Gate of Fuling Imperial Tomb demonstrates strict hierarchy system of ancient China and profound intelligence attached to every part of the building. Even a gate is full of mysteries and implications. Of the three doors, the middle one called the "Door of Spirit" for access of spirits of the buried, only opened when such sacrificial objects as sacrificial boards, ceremonious silk embroideries and golden and silver foils were carried in by the officials concerned through this door. This door is honored by ancient people with awe and regarded as a taboo. For example, when Emperors, Empresses or other court officials passed by the gate, the gate should be covered with reed mat and they were afraid to peep inside. The door in the east side is called "Door of Emperor," which is access for Emperors to offer sacrifices; and the one in the west is called "Door of Officials." Shih Tsu Fu Lin's Facts of Qing Dynasty stipulates, "When sacrifices are offered to Fuling Imperial Tomb and Zhaoling Imperial Tomb, Emperor shall enter the left door (east side) with his body bending to show his respect, officials enter through the right door (west side), and sacrificial offerings shall be carried in through the door in the center." However, in practice, the specific implementation can be "flexible."

清东陵（孝陵）／左下图 East Qing Mausoleum (Xiao Mausoleum) / Lower Left
清西陵（慕陵）／左上图 West Qing Mausoleum (Mu Mausoleum) / Upper Left
正红门"三太极"琉璃斗栱／右图 Glazed Triadic Dougongs (corbel bracket) on Front Red Gate / Right
正红门西侧南向的五彩琉璃壁［长11.9米，高约5米］／右页图
South-facing Glazed Wall on the West Side of Front Red Gate (11.9 meters long, 5 meters high) / Right Page

琉璃龙壁上的工名

站在大红门前面，就可以看见大红门东西两侧墙上都镶嵌有蟠龙五彩琉璃壁，因为它的位置如同衣服的袖子开在两边，故又称"袖壁"，也叫"龙砖看壁"，西侧袖壁的龙是黑色，东侧袖壁的龙是绿色。福陵里仅有四个龙壁，除了正红门，东西红门都没有，物以稀为贵，比起昭陵里十二个龙壁，福陵的四个龙壁尤显珍贵。永陵虽然也有四个龙壁，但是与福陵的龙壁材质不同，是砖雕的。福陵袖壁两边是围绕陵寝的高墙，下有石基，上用青砖砌成，墙顶用黄色琉璃构件装饰，早晨阳光初照，金光灿然夺目，而金瓦红墙使福陵显得更加庄严宏伟。因为墙前面覆红土，故又称此墙为"红墙"、"红城"或"风水红墙"。关外三陵中，只有永陵没有风水红墙。而据说福陵里每一个建筑部件上都采用"实名制"，即每个工匠都要对自己的产品负责。在袖壁上可以清晰地看到这些建筑上的符号，修建时也是按照这些编号将它们安放在指定的位置，并都标有时间和名字。隆恩殿的台基石料的背面就标有东南西北的字样，只是没有刻在正面。历史上，秦始皇陵兵马俑身上和建筑的砖上都留有清晰的人名印章，到明孝陵砖上也有，说明清朝完全地继承了中华民族的文化传统。

正红门是琉璃斗栱装饰，古建筑中，木质斗栱是起到一个支撑的类似"弹簧"的作用的，而琉璃斗栱仅仅是用作装饰，清帝陵中只有福陵和昭陵才有，相传是山西侯氏家族烧制，也是这两陵的一大特色，至高无上。在欣赏福陵精致细腻的斗栱时，我无意间发现了一个分外眼熟的小巧三太极，这个雕刻由红黄蓝三色流云相生环绕而成。多少次我来此作画拍摄，却都与它擦肩而过，并不曾留意过这个图案，多少年来它安静地隐匿在世人纷繁的视线之外，这次终于被我捕捉进镜头之中，也激起了我对于往事的回忆。

说起我和它的缘分，开始于我在朝鲜半岛游历之时，三太极是那里常见的一种图案。第二次遇见，是在日本的博物馆里，看见了一块瓦当，是江户时期（18—19世纪）的，学名叫"三巴纹轩栈瓦"，原来日本人给这个图案起名为"三巴纹"。后来行至日本许多地方，越是能够看见它的身影，或是出现在众多神社的建筑物装饰之中，或是显现于日本的文物、和服之上。

第三次巧遇之时，我在东日本桥住所的北面是一个著名的今户神社，里面供奉的是为我们中国人所熟知的招财猫，我经常从那里路过，久而久之，和神社的神主——市野智慧渐渐熟稔，她给我表演了正规的法式，还特意让我拍照以留纪念。在这里，我看见三太极这个图腾遍布神社，无论是法器、饰物上，还是建筑和服装上，那是她们家族的家纹，被绣在衣服两侧的胸口和后领口处，充满了神秘的

东红门石雕 / 上图
Stone Carving of East Red Gate / Upper

东红门 [长 10.11 米，宽 8.37 米，高 13 米] / 右图
East Red Gate (10.11 meters long, 8.37 meters wide, 13 meters high) /Right

意味。

而现在，居然在福陵的正红门之上第四次与它邂逅，时空的交叠让我产生了深深的好奇，为什么这里也会有这个神秘的图案呢？

讲到太极这个图腾，中国人最熟悉不过。早在上古时候，伏羲上观星辰，下观地理，取象于宇宙万物而创八卦；后来宋朝陈抟在先人的基础之上，将八卦中抽象的思维用阴阳鱼的方式表现出来，阴阳相调，同生互补，是为我们今天所看到的太极八卦图。这个图腾所具有的丰富思想内涵使得它流传千年而愈加深远，从此以后成为华夏子孙认知程度最高的一种民族图腾。

既然是中国特有的古老图腾，那么三太极出现在福陵的雕刻之中自然是合情合理，怎么又会隔山越海，出现在朝鲜半岛和日本呢？我联想到，努尔哈赤的祖先——肇祖元皇帝现在还葬在朝鲜，目前永陵里他的墓穴不过是个衣冠冢，想必生前是和朝鲜有着一些渊源的，会不会是用三太极来体现一种对祖辈的怀念之情呢？

对着镜头里的三太极，我心里终于一片澄澈，谜题如果都被平铺直叙地展现在世人面前，哪里还有那么多的奇妙想法和浪漫思绪？只需透过这一块小小的三太极而感受到中华文化的厚重，就已足矣。

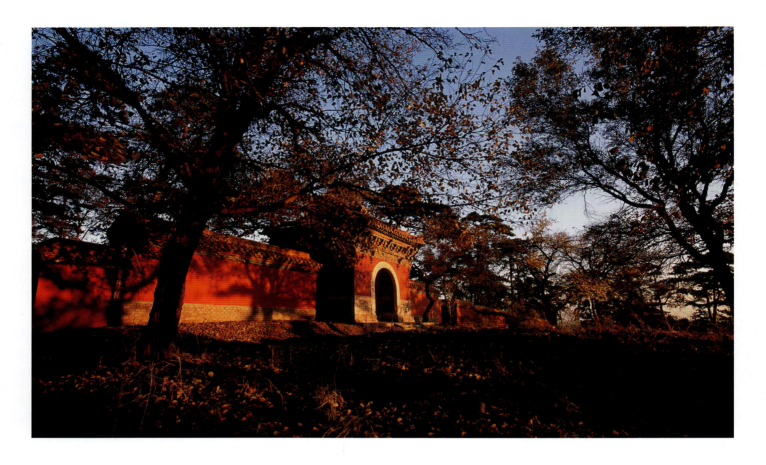

SIGNATURE OF CRAFTSMEN ON GLAZED COILED DRAGON WALL

Standing in front of Front Red Gate, you can see the walls on its both sides decorated with colorfully-glazed coiled dragons. Because the walls look like a pair of sleeves of clothes, they are also called "sleeve wall" or "dragon brick screen wall," of which the west dragon is black and the east one is green. There are only four dragon walls at the front red gate of Fuling Imperial Tomb. The four dragon walls are more precious than the twelve in Zhaoling Imperial Tomb. There are also four dragon walls in Yong Mausoleum, but they are carved out of bricks. On both sides of the sleeves walls, there are walls of blue bricks surrounding the Mausoleum, which are supported by stone base. The top of the walls is decorated with yellow glazed components, shining in the early morning sun. The golden tiles and red walls leave a touch of grandeur and majesty to Fuling Imperial Tomb. Red earth is painted on the surface of walls, so it is also known as "Red Wall," "Red City Wall" or "geomantic red wall." It is said that every component of Fuling Imperial Tomb adopts a "real name system," that is, each craftsman must be responsible for his own products. Marks of such signs are clearly seen on sleeve walls. The components were arranged in strict order as they were designated to be placed in specified location marked with date and name. The back sides of base stones of Hall of Eminent Favor (also Long'en Hall, name of building, used for dead Emperor) are engraved with East, West, South and North, but nothing can be seen from its front side. In history, names and seals were clearly marked on Terracotta Warriors and Horses, and bricks of Mausoleum of Qin Shihuang while those marks were also found on bricks of Xiao Mausoleum of Ming Dynasty, from which we know that Qing Dynasty had well inherited traditional Chinese cultures.

Front Red Gate is decorated with glazed brackets, which are used to support like "springs" in ancient architecture. However, the brackets here is just for decoration, which can be found only in Fu and Zhaoling Imperial Tombs among Qing mausoleums. It is said such brackets as a typical feature of the two mausoleums were produced by a Hou family in Shanxi Province. In appreciation of the exquisite and delicate brackets of Fuling Imperial Tomb, I accidentally found a three-colored Taiji pattern, which is a sculpture with the red, yellow and blue colors winding side by side. For numerous times, I have been coming here to draw pictures and take photos, but I never noticed this pattern before. This pattern has hidden itself from noisy sights for so many years, but now it is captured in my camera, which arouses my old memories.

Talking about the stories of three-colored Taiji pattern, I first acquainted myself with it when I traveled in Korean Peninsula, which was a common pattern over there. The second time I saw the pattern was when I visited a museum in Japan. It was a piece of eave tile named "Sam Pamun Pattern Pantile" in E-do Era (18-19 century), and then I knew its Japanese name as "Sam Pamum Pattern." In later time, the more places I visited in Japan, the more I saw this pattern. The pattern is usually decorated on the buildings of shrines or appears on Japanese antiques or kimonos.

The third time I saw three-colored Taiji pattern was in Imado Shrine, north of Higashi Nihonbashi, where I lived in Tokyo. Inside the Shrine, Fortune Cat, well known in China, is worshiped. I often went by the shrine and naturally I made friends with the shrine master, Tomoe Ichino. She performed the formal religious ceremony for me and gave me special permission to take pictures. Here, I saw the totem of three-colored Taiji everywhere in the shrine. The patterns on dharma vessels, accessories, clothing and buildings are her family patterns, which are embroidered on both sides of the chest and back of collar, displaying a message of mystery.

But now, for the fourth time I see it on Front Red Gate of Fuling Imperial Tomb. The overlapping of time and space is arousing my curiosity. Why is there such a mysterious pattern?

As for Taiji totem, Chinese knows better. Back in ancient times, Fuxi created Eight Trigrams on concepts of sky and earth, nature and society; later in Song Dynasty, Chen Tuan manifested the abstract theory of Eight Trigrams with Yin Yang fish based on the understandings of former thinkers. This is the Picture of the Ultimate and Eight Trigrams we have today, with yin and yang depending on each other and complementing each other. This totem has rich ideological contents and makes it spread even more far-reaching in the last Millennium and now it is one of the most acknowledged totems of Chinese people.

Since it is a unique totem of ancient Chinese culture, it's natural that the carved three-colored Taiji pattern appears in Fuling Imperial Tomb. But how come the pattern is popular in Korean Peninsula and Japan? I think of Nurhaci's ancestors, the Founding Emperor, whose tomb is still now in North Korea. The tomb now in Yong Mausoleum is only a cenotaph.

There might be some relations with North Korea when he was alive. Is it possible that the three-colored Taiji pattern is used to commemorate ancestors?

Gazing at Taiji I captured in my camera, I calm down finally. If the puzzle is plainly explained, where would so many wonderful ideas and romantic thoughts come from? It suffices to experience the rich Chinese culture through this little three-colored Taiji pattern.

西红门西侧／左页图
Western Side of West Red Gate / Left Page
[长10.11米，宽8.37米，高13米]
(10.11 meters long, 8.37 meters wide, 13 meters high)

西红门东侧／下图
Eastern Side of West Red Gate / Lower

红门内东华表／左图
East-side Huabiao inside Red Gate / Left
红门外西华表／下图
West-side Huabiao outside Red Gate / Lower

粗犷的华表

福陵里，还有一种建筑是比较吸引我的，那就是华表。华表，是中国一种传统的建筑形式，既有道路标志的作用，又有为过路行人留言的作用。据考，华表在原始社会的尧舜时代就出现了。晋代崔豹在《古今注·问答释义》中说："程雅问曰：'尧设诽谤之木，何也？'答曰：'今之华表木也。以横木交柱头，状若花也，形似桔槔，大路交衢悉施焉。或谓之表木，以表王者纳谏也，亦以表识路衢也。'"可见当时的华表为木制，其作用可以让人进谏，书写人们对时弊的观点、看法，供王者采纳；也可以标明路衢，指示交通，相当于今天的路标、道路指示牌。后来的邮亭、传舍也用它作标识，名叫"桓木"或"表木"，后又统称为"桓木"，因为古代的"桓"与"华"音相近，所以慢慢读成了"华表"。

华表的质变是从秦始皇开始的，它由木变石，从广为民用到皇家独享，由告示牌变成了帝王柱、皇权标。从秦始皇开始，华表一般采用最坚硬的花岗石打造，头上常盘踞雄狮，周身缠绕蟠龙，完全成了一种专制集权的象征。今日的华表也是一种标志性建筑，它已经成为中华民族的象征之一。我从事品牌学研究，设计了《中国品牌年鉴》的标志，就是以华表为造型。昭陵华表比福陵建得要晚，是乾隆时建的，石材比较细腻，从美学角度考虑，昭陵的华表造型也比福陵的更加优美。关外三陵中，永陵没有华表，福陵的华表，是清未入关之前修建的，无论是选材还是建造比例比之昭陵华表都显得粗犷，工艺上略逊一筹，不是很完美。而关内清陵的华表，则都雕刻得精美绝伦，美轮美奂，无论是材质还是技法，都比关外要强出很多。

清福陵总共有六根华表，分别在大门口，石路口和石路末。华表用于宫殿、陵寝外的道路两旁，也称为神道柱、擎天柱、石望柱、万云柱，表，标或碣。福陵的华表只有左侧那一根下面的小石兽是完整的，其他华表上的石兽的头部都被齐刷刷地砍下，据说是毁于"文化大革命"时期。据《清世祖实录》记载，这些"华表"建造于顺治七年（1650年），

虽然石柱的样式并不完全相同，因为康雍乾至嘉庆各朝都有重修，但就其结构来说，大都由底座、护栏、柱体、云版、天盘、栏顶、顶兽等部分组成。

福陵的华表，其底座是三层莲花座，柱体为八角形，通体浮雕云纹及龙蟠柱，顶部横插有云板，上面各刻一"日""月"字（东端华表刻有"日"字，西端的刻有"月"字）。关于这两个日月，有人说，清朝把这两个字分开刻是寓意把"明"朝分开。个人认为，身为统治者的胸襟不会那么狭隘。古代皇帝都自命"天子"，取"与天齐寿，日月同辉"之意更有道理。华表顶部是"天盘"，上有坐犼一只，样子似犬非犬，身有麟甲，长尾与鬃发相连，浑身瘦骨嶙峋，作昂首跷尾弓颈高鸣状。古人说：犼"似犬，食人"。由于此兽猛烈异常，所以刻在石柱上要它守陵。据说这种石兽，性好望，相传设置在宫殿前而犼头向内的，名叫"望君出"，是希望皇帝不要深居宫廷，而要经常出来看看自己的百姓臣民，体恤民情；犼头向外的，名叫"望君归"，是希望皇帝外出巡视后就马上回来，不要迷恋山水玩乐，快回来治理国家。

BOLD AND UNSTRAINED HUABIAO

Another building attraction in Fuling Imperial Tomb is huabiao, an ornamental pillar or marble column erected in front of palaces or tombs. It is a traditional Chinese architectural form, which functions not only as a road sign but also as a message bulletin for passengers. According to research, huabiao appeared in the times of Yao and Shun in the primitive society. In "Annotations by Questions and Answers" of Gujinzhu (Notes to Things Old and New by Cui Bao in Jin Dynasty), "Cheng Ya asked: 'What is Yao's defamation wood?' Answered: 'It's today's huabiao wood, which is constructed by putting a horizontal bar on the top of a column to form a pattern like flower in shape of shaduf. They are erected on main roads and at crossings. It is also called expressing wood, which not only shows that King is open to public opinions, but also indicates directions of roads.'" It is obvious that huabiao was made of wood then whose functions are to welcome suggestions and opinions on politics for king's reference and to show the way which direction passengers should take, equivalent to today's road signs. The later postal kiosks and guest houses also adopted such pillar as an identity, known as "Huanmu" (postal pillar) or "Biaomu" (identifying pillar), but later generally referred to as "Huanmu." "Huanmu" slowly developed into "Huabiao" because of their similar pronunciation.

The essential change of huabiaos took place from the First Emperor of Qin Dynasty. The building material was then changed from wood to stone, and its use was passed on for exclusive use of royal family with the function shifting from message bulletin to imperial pillar. From Qin Shihuang, huabiao was made of the hardest granite, often with entrenched lion on its top and dragon coiling around the pillar, which were completely changed to symbol of tyrannical central-

ization. However, huabiao is only a typical Chinese architectural form in today's China, which is now one of the most important logos of China. I specialize in brand research, and the logo I designed for Chinese Brands Yearbook takes as its prototype huabiao of Zhaoling Imperial Tomb, because, I think, it was built with finer stones in the years of Emperor Qianlong and later than that of Fuling Imperial Tomb, and also, much more beautiful than that of Fuling Imperial Tomb from an aesthetic point of view. There are no huabiao in Yong Mausoleum, and huabiao in Fuling Imperial Tomb was built before their entry into Central Plain at Shanhai Pass, so that either selection of its building materials or proportion of its construction is rougher than that in Zhaoling Imperial Tomb, and not perfect due to its slightly inferior workmanship. However, Huabiaos of the mausoleums inside Shanhai Pass are exquisitely carved, which are much better in terms of both materials and techniques.

There are totally 6 huabiaos at Fuling Imperial Tomb, located at the front gate, the beginning and end of stone path. Huabiao was used on sides of roads outside palaces or mausoleums, also known as spirit-path pillar, sky-holding pillar, gazing stone pillar, thousand-cloud pillar, biao, sign, or tablet. Only the small little animal on base of the left-side huabiao at the beginning of the stone path in Fuling Imperial Tomb is preserved intact while heads of other animals are said to have been cut away during the Cultural Revolution. According to Shih Tsu Fu Lin's Facts of Qing Dynasty, these huabiaos were built in the 7th ruling year of Emperor Shunzhi (1650). The shapes of these pillars are not completely the same, because they were renovated from the years of Emperor Qianlong to the years of Emperor Jiaqing. However, construction of huabiaos generally consists of such parts as base seat, guard rail, pillar body, cloud board, sky dish, column capital, and top animals.

The base of huabiao in Fuling Imperial Tomb is of three-layer lotus. The pillar body is of octagonal shape engraved with relief moire and coiled dragon, and on its top a cloud board is inserted in the pillar with Chinese character Ri (日, sun) or Yue (月, month) engraved on the eastern or western side respectively. It is said that the separation of these two characters Ri or Yue indicates Ming (明) Dynasty was broken up by Qing Dynasty. In my own opinion, it's unnecessary to be so narrow-minded as a new ruling power. In ancient China, Emperors usually proclaim themselves as "Son of Heaven," which means "live as long as heaven, as bright as the Sun and the Moon." This explanation is much more reasonable than the above one. On top of Huabiao, there is a capital, on which sits a Sky Roaring Hou, a legendary animal which looks like a dog, covered with scales on its bony body, tail and mane hair attached together, raising his head and tail, roaring fiercely towards sky. The ancient thought: Hou, "resembles dog, but eats man." As the animal is ferocious, it is usually engraved on stone column to defend mausoleums. It is said such animals have a habit of gazing at the sky. According to legends, the head of Hou put in front of palaces looking inward is called Wangjunchu, (望君出, see Emperor go out) warning Emperor against indulging in pleasure and urging him to go to people for their complaints; while the head of Hou looking outward is called Wangjungui, (望君归, see Emperor return) warning Emperor against staying too long outside palaces and urging him to return in due time and work for his country.

红门内东华表／左页图
East-side Huabiao inside Red Gate / Left Page
清东陵（景陵）华表／上图
Huabiao of East Qing Mausoleum (Jing Mausoleum) /Upper

东侧老虎石象生／左上图
East-side Stone Tiger Statue / Upper Left
清东陵（景陵）石象生／右上图
Stone Statue of East Qing Mausoleum (Jing Mausoleum) / Upper Right

罕见的老虎石象生

在华表中间神道两旁有一组石兽群，它们由北依次是石骆驼、石马、石虎、石狮，共计四对，而永陵中没有设置石象生，昭陵则有六对石象生，是关外三陵中，石象生数量最多的。其全部用青色岩石雕琢，基座为大理石，须弥式，上面雕有"锦袱"，锦袱四角各坠古钱一枚，须弥座上雕有花纹。石兽如同一批"卫士"护卫着皇陵。据说石马是仿当年努尔哈赤乘坐的蒙古马形象雕刻而成。其实，在神道两侧置放石人石兽的做法由来已久。相传秦朝有一名大力士，名阮翁仲，他身长一丈三尺，异于常人，力大无比。曾驻守临洮，征服匈奴有功。阮翁仲死后，秦始皇十分怀念他，特制其铜像立于咸阳宫司马门外。据说匈奴人来咸阳，见到铜人，竟以为是活着的阮翁仲，吓得落荒而逃。从此，人们便把宫阙或陵寝前的铜人、石人称为"翁仲"，也叫"石象生"、"石翁仲"。《封氏闻见记》（注解9）记载："墓上树柏、路头狮虎、魉象俱之"。故墓前立狮虎陵区种松柏。这些勇猛彪悍的石兽极驯服地守护在陵寝前，既是墓主人身份地位等级的标志，也有驱邪、镇墓的含义，更无疑会增强陵寝的威严和神秘之感。

关于福陵石象生设置的时间，《太宗实录》天聪八年己丑条的记载："礼部和硕贝勒萨哈廉传谕工部曰：太祖山陵建寝殿、植松木、立石狮、石象、石虎、石马、石驼等，又方古制行之。"然而萨哈廉的"传谕"仅仅是按"古制"的提议，并未立即实行；这些石兽的正式建造时间是顺治七年之后。对此清《世祖实录》有明确记载：顺治七年四月乙酉，立福陵"卧骆驼、立马、坐狮、坐虎各一对"。不过，因为历经几代，顺治年建的石象生也破损严重，后来康熙、乾隆等东临祭祖，又重新修过，所以，细心人会发现石象生的基座和上部分石头的颜色不同，有人认为，起初，褔陵石兽的下部没有石座。

因为早期此陵规模较小，石兽与陵寝其他建筑的体量比例必须协调，这些石座是顺治十六年因为增修方城、角楼等整体建筑而增加的。所以福陵石兽是顺治七年和十六年两次建造的。

我个人认为这是乾隆皇帝给加的底座。福陵、昭陵里的石象生，在这点上是相同的，就是底座和上部分的石质，石色都不一致。老虎，狮子，马和神龟流泪都是材质一样的石料，据此可推断是一个时代的。不过，昭陵里的大象和马的雕像与底座材质都一致，不是同一时期雕的。比较之下，昭陵中没有老虎，虎是福陵中独有的，甚至可以说是历代陵寝中唯一的。二十多年来，我一直试图把老虎石象生拍得精彩，但是那些年，要么冬天，虎头上覆盖着积雪，耳朵与雪连起来，老虎看起来更像一只举起右手的招财猫，要么夏天树影斑驳，使它看起来是一只"花斑虎"，就在我接到此书"列入国家十二五规划"的通知时，我再去福陵拍摄，石象生周围的树已经长得密密匝匝的，叶与叶之间没有空隙，恰巧只有一束光穿过树荫，照在虎头上，似乎是上天特意为我拍摄而打的光。终于，我拍到了一张光线较好的老虎石象生照片，仿佛天赐，同事说老虎的表情可爱得像动画片里的机器猫。

福陵里没有石象，这是因为皇太极给努尔哈赤修建陵寝的时候，还没有统一南方，对汉文化也不是很了解，所以没有见过大象，但是后人给皇太极修建昭陵的时候，清朝已经进关，对汉文化的认识进一步加深了，就在石象生中加进了大象。而后修时所用的材料都是从山海关南运来的，因为东北没有汉白玉这种石材。神龟流泪的石材与石象生青色石头都是以前就有的，上面都带有砂眼。关内的石象生，属清东陵孝陵的规模最大，共有18对，而泰陵雍正时因为风水的问题曾不设置石象生，后来到乾隆十三年（1748），乾隆帝为了彰显对祖先的孝道又恢复了设置，其间还引起了他与臣工抵牾的波折。其实乾隆皇帝一直想给自己的陵寝修石象生，但是因为他父亲雍正帝陵寝中没有石象生，所以他就想出了补建这个办法，不仅如此，关外三陵中很多石象生底座也是乾隆皇帝给补加的。关外石象生，虽然在石材上不如关内，但是在雕刻技法上却更加生动逼真，看起来如真的一样。关内的石象生，则更强调皇权与威严，多了文臣武将的石像，动物都是卑躬屈膝的，如跪着的大象，不得不佩服古人，将至高无上演绎到如此程度。

雪漫福陵骆驼石象生／左页图
Stone Camel Statue Covered with Snow in Fuling Imperial Tomb／Left Page
黑色的福陵骆驼石象生与灰色的清东陵骆驼石象生／上图
Black Stone Camel Statue in Fuling Imperial Tomb and Gray Stone Camel Statue in East Qing Mausoleum／Upper

RARE TIGER STONE STATUES

There are a group of stone animal statues on both sides of Spirit Path among huabiaos. From north to south, they are stone camels, horses, tigers and lions, totally four pairs. There aren't any animal statues in Yong Mausoleum while in Zhaoling Imperial Tomb there are six pairs of animal statues. All the statues are carved out of grey stones on patterned Sumeru-throne marble base, upon which a colorful scarf is engraved with two coins hanging on its four corners. They guard the Mausoleum as "guardians." It is said that stone horses imitate the image of Mongolian horse that Nurhaci rode. In fact, the practice of placing stone statues on both sides of the spiritual path dates back long in history. According to legends, there was a strong man named Yuan Wengzhong in Qin Dynasty, who was nearly 3 meters tall and as strong as a horse, quite different from ordinary people. He once was stationed in Lintao, and distinguished himself in defeating Huns. After Yuan Wengzhong's death, Qin Shihuang ordered to build a bronze statue of him at Sima Gate of Xianyang Palace to commemorate him. It is said that when Huns came to Xianyang, they mistook the bronze as Yuan Wengzhong alive, and fled away in great horror. From then on, bronze or stone statues in front of palaces or mausoleums were called "Wengzhong," also know as "Stone Warrior" or "Stone Wengzhong." Records of What Feng Saw and Heard (Note 9) reads: "Cypress trees around tombs, and statues of lion and tiger at crossroads drive monsters and ghosts away." Thus, lions and tigers are erected in front of tombs and cypress trees are planted in surrounding burial areas. These fierce and valiant stone guarding animals tamely stand in front of mausoleums, which not only are sign of supreme status but also contain meanings of expelling evil spirits and protecting mausoleums, and thus undoubtedly enhance atmospheres of majesty and mystery.

The installation time of stone animal statues in Fuling Imperial Tomb is recorded in the 26th entry of the 8th ruling year of Emperor Tiancong in Chronicles of Hong Taiji: "Heshuo Baylor Sahalian, who was in charge of Ministry of Rites, ordered Ministry of Works to build burial palace, plant cypress trees, erect stone lions, elephants, tigers, horses and camels on Hong Taiji's mausoleum hill, just following the traditional practice." However, the order of Sahalian to follow the traditional practice wasn't put into practice; the formal construction of these stone statues was carried out in the 7th ruling year of Emperor Shunzhi. This was clearly recorded in Shih Tsu Fu Lin's Facts of Qing Dynasty: on April 22 of the 7th ruling year of Emperor Shunzhi, "each pair of crouching camels, standing horses, crouching lions and tigers were installed" in Fuling Imperial Tomb. However, after several generations, stone statues built in the years of Shunzhi experienced serious damage. They were renovated when Emperor Kangxi and Qianlong came to offer sacrifices to their ancestors. Careful visitors may find that colors of the base and body of the stone statue are different. Some people think that there weren't stone bases under the stone statues. At the beginning, the scale of Mausoleum was comparatively small; accordingly, proportion of the stone statues must coordinate with other buildings. The stone bases were added later when Square City and turrets were built. So the stones animal statues were built and renovated at different times, that is, the 7th and 16th ruling year of Emperor Shunzhi.

I personally think that the stone bases were added by Emperor Qianlong. The stone animal statues of Fuling Imperial Tomb and Zhaoling Imperial Tomb are the same in this aspect, i.e. the stone color of the bases is different from that of statue body. The

狮子石象生／左页图
Stone Lion Statue / Left Page
清东陵（孝陵）狮子石象生／上图
Stone Lion Statute of East Qing Mausoleum (Xiao Mausoleum) / Upper

清东陵（孝陵）卧马石象生／上图
Lying Stone Horse Statue of East Qing Mausoleum (Xiao Mausoleum) / Upper

立马石象生／右图
Standing Stone Horse Statue / Right

stone materials of tiger, lion, horse and tear-shedding turtle are the same, from which we can infer that they were made at the same time. However, the material of statue bodies of elephant and horse in Zhaoling Imperial Tomb is different from that of the base, so they were not made at the same time. In contrast, there aren't tigers in Zhaoling Imperial Tomb, and tigers only appear in Fuling Imperial Tomb. We can even say that they are the only stone tiger statues in ancient mausoleums. For the last twenty years, I have been trying to take wonderful pictures for these tiger stone statues; however, the tiger head is either covered with snow in winter, making the tigers look like Fortune Cats with a lift-up right hands, or the mottled tree shadows make them look like "spotted tigers" in summer. I paid another visit to Fuling Imperial Tomb for pictures right after I received notice that this book is listed in the "Twelfth Five-Year National Plan." The trees around the stone statues were very dense, leaving no space among the leaves, but it happened that a beam of light fell on the tiger's head through the shade of a tree, as if it was meant for me to shoot. Fortunately, I got a considerably good picture of the tiger stone statue with right exposure as if it were a gift from heaven. My colleagues said that the face of the tiger is as cute as Doraemon in cartoons.

There is no elephant statur in Fuling Imperial Tomb. This is because Hong Taiji's construction of Mausoleum for Nurhaci was carried out before unification of the south, and they didn't know much then about Han culture and never saw an elephant. But when Mausoleum of Hong Taiji was built, his descendents knew more about Han culture after they came to the southern side of Shanhai Pass, and therefore stone elephant was added to Zhaoling Imperial Tomb. Materials used for later renovation were shipped from the south of Shanhai Pass, because there isn't white marble in the Northeast. The grey stone materials of Tear-shedding Turtle and stone animal statues were old ones because there are tiny holes on them. As for the stone animal statues outside the Shanhai Pass, Xiao Mausoleum has the largest scale, with 18 pairs in all. There aren't such statues in Tai Mausoleum of Emperor Yongzheng due to certain geomantic reasons. But later in the 13th ruling year (1748) of Emperor Qianlong, he restored the construction of stone animal statues, which had caused contradictory anecdotes between Emperor and his officials. In fact, Emperor Qianlong wanted to build stone statues in his own mausoleum, but there were no statues in his father's mausoleum. So he came up with the idea to restore stone statues in his father Yongzheng's Mausoleum. He also added bases to many stone statues in Three Mausoleums outside Shanhai Pass. Although materials used for those stone statues are not as good as those inside Shanhai Pass, their carving technique are more vivid, which help make the statues look like the real animals. However, the stone statues inside the Pass lay more emphasis on imperial power and majesty, in which kneeling animals such as elephants, together with the obsequious officials, illustrate the supreme power to the unprecedented level.

神道／右页图
Spirit Path / Right Page
[全长566米]
(566 meters long)

灵魂之道——神道

在福陵大红门以内,有三条笔直的石铺甬路,垂直北上,南起正红门,正中与"神门"相连,北至隆恩殿后,全长566米,陵寝古建筑均以其为中轴线对称分布,平面布局规整,层次分明,这就是福陵神道。关于神道,顾名思义就是神行的道路,又称天道,语出《易经》(注解10)"观天之神道,而四时不忒,圣人以神道设教,而天下服矣"。把神道当作墓道使用是汉代以后的事,"墓前开道,建石柱以为标",汉代大将霍去病的神道是目前被发现的最早的神道。在福陵中,三条石路从东至西分别叫作、君道、神道、臣道。中间的神道和正红门只有在棺椁入陵和祭祀抬供桌祭品时才打开,并从此关闭,东边是君王拜祭时走的通道,现在却作为游客入口。今天,在很多关于清代的电视剧中,我们都可以看到皇帝在两陵祭祖的镜头,其中,皇帝总是气宇轩昂,威风凛凛,甚至是大摇大摆地走在了正中的神道上。而君道和臣道上,也依次站满了身着朝服的大臣。每当看到这种场面,我都想,这不仅是人们关于历史的无知,也是因为想当然而犯的错误。可能除了研究历史的人,很少有人会去思考,甚至微微想一想,这三条同样细长的小道,究竟是做什么的,是简单的装饰还是别有用意?而在清朝,对于神道的使用可是有着极其严格的规定与惩罚,特别是靠近碑楼附近的神道,有"横走罚,竖走杀,马过砍蹄"的规矩。而现在,普通百姓却可以随便走,我在感叹社会进步的同时,不免也感慨世事的沧海桑田,往日帝王的威严与权威,都湮没在历史的尘嚣中,只有这些无声的建筑,依然。

SPIRIT PATH

Inside Great Red Gate of Fuling Imperial Tomb, there are three straight gravel paths, leading to the north vertically. The roads start from Front Red Gate with its center passing through "Door of Spirit" and ends at the rear part of Eminent Favor Hall, covering a distance of 566 meters. Layout of ancient mausoleum building is symmetrical with an axle in the center, orderly and neatly organized, with distinct gradation – the axle is Spirit Path of Fuling Imperial Tomb. Spirit Path, as the name implies, is the road for spirits of the deceased, which is also called "Divine Road."

"Divine Road" is quoted from Book of Changes (Note 10). "If you watch Divine Road, you'll find it keeps its normal appearance throughout the year; so if sages set Spirit Path, people will follow it". Taking Divine Road as tomb passage was popular after Han Dynasty. "Open a road in front the tomb and build a stone pillar as the landmark" – Spirit Path of the tomb of Huo Qubing, General of Han Dynasty, is considered as the earliest one till now. In Fuling Imperial Tomb of Qing Dynasty, three stone roads from the left to the right are called in proper order: Emperor's Path, Spirit Path, and Official Path. Spirit Path in the middle and Front Red Gate were only opened when coffins or sacrifices were carried in and then closed. The left path, Emperor's Path, is for Emperors to walk on to salute the dead. The right path, Official Path, is now for visitors to walk on. Nowadays, in many TV series related to Qing Dynasty, we can see the scene that Emperors worship ancestors in the two mausoleums. Emperors present themselves impressively with a majestic look, swinging along the road in the middle, while Emperor's Path and Official Path are lined with ministers in court dress. I would think it is due to lack of knowledge about history that people act this way and they took it for granted. Except for those who study history, very few people would think over this question. They may not even think of it: What are the purposes of the three narrow paths? Is it simply a decoration or for other intentions? In Qing Dynasty, there were strict regulations and punishment rules over the use of Spirit Path, especially Spirit Path close to the stele pavilion, which is forbidden to walk on: "People who cross it will be punished and those track it will be killed. Horses' hoofs will be cut if they pass by." Nowadays, ordinary people can walk on it freely. The society is making progress, while time brings significant changes to the world and the emperor's dignity and power all submerged into an uproar of history. However, these silent buildings stand as usual.

神桥／左页图、上图 Spirit Bridge / Left Page, Upper
[约宽6.98米，上神桥长约13米，下神桥长约25.6米]
(about 6.98 meters wide, with its upper Bridge 13 meters long and lower Bridge 25.6 meters long)

使人卑躬屈膝的神桥

福陵有两座神桥，分上下两个桥洞，建在一百单八蹬两端。神桥均是单孔拱形桥，桥两旁有扶手墙，高1.2米，青砖砌成，用黄色琉璃瓦封顶。一般皇陵神桥都修得十分讲究，涵洞、桥身、护栏、望柱等都雕刻得很细致，相对来说，福陵神桥比其他神桥显得朴实无华。此桥桥面从前也是砖石铺面，今已改成"品"字形铺设的方石。福陵神桥的桥洞与桥身都是拱形的，过桥的时候，必须卑躬屈膝才能顺利通过，这也是设计者用建筑诠释权力与威严的一种方式，不能不令人感叹古人的智慧。河北清代陵内的拱桥一般都是平的，这是因为道光帝觉得愧对天下百姓，无颜再受后人拜谒，不过关内的清陵中一般都有金水桥，甚至类似正红门那样等级森严的神桥、君桥、臣桥，而关外三陵中，则没有那么多桥，这可能与地形也有一定关系，关内清陵神桥下一般都有较大的天然水域，而关外三陵则没有，一般都是人工水域。福陵神桥在红门里，我一直以为永陵没有神桥，后来发现永陵也有神桥，在第一道栅栏门那儿，有一个一尺宽的沟，桥不易被发现。而昭陵神桥在红门外，至于为什么也修成平的，至今让我费解。

　　神桥，顾名思义，就是建在神道之上的桥。福陵神桥的两个桥洞，第一个是旱桥，下面无水，是象征性的，桥上的桥洞用于排水。神桥是清朝帝王陵寝中普遍使用的建筑形式，它既有装饰陵寝建筑的作用，更有其实用价值。神桥用来保护陵寝免受雨水侵蚀，陵内有一些人工或自然形成的排水沟（又叫"龙须沟"）、神桥其实就是架在神道上的排水桥函。关于福陵的神桥，从前，每到雨季，山水汇集下来，从神桥自西而东流出。因神桥地势很高，从远处遥望神桥，有如一瀑布高悬空中，也如当空飘起一束银白的绸带，颇为壮观，形成了著名的福陵景观之一。

神桥／左图、右上图 Spirit Bridge / Left, Upper Right
[神桥总高 6.09 米，桥洞高 3.01 米，宽 4.02 米]
(6.09 meters high with its arch 3.01 meters high and 4.02 meters wide)
清西陵（泰陵）神桥／右下图
Spirit Bridge of West Qing Mausoleum (Tai Mausoleum) / Lower Right

SPIRIT BRIDGE, WHICH ONE HAS TO BOW WHEN CROSSING ON IT

There are two spirit bridges in Fuling Imperial Tomb, with two bridge holes, one upside and one downside, which are built at the two ends of 108 Steps. Both bridges are single-hole arched, with the handrail walls on both sides, which is 1.2 meters high, built with black bricks and yellow glazed tiles on top. Generally speaking, imperial spirit bridge is particular, and its tunnels, body of bridge, handrail and baluster column are all carved with delicate designs. Comparatively speaking, Spirit Bridge of Fuling Imperial Tomb is simpler than others. The bridge surface is paved with black bricks, which now have been changed into block stones. The bridge openings and body are all in arch shape. One must watch his or her head when passing through it. It is also a method used by its designers to render supremacy and power of the dignity, from which we can read wisdom of ancient people. The arch bridges of Qing Dynasty inside Hebei Province are generally flat, because Emperor Daoguang of Qing Dynasty felt that he did not deserve respect from his civilians. Generally speaking, there are Golden Water Bridges in the mausoleums of Qing Dynasty, and there are even spirit bridges, emperor bridges and official bridges, which are symbols of hierarchy. But there aren't so many bridges in Three Mausoleums outside Shanhai Pass. The terrains may matter in the differences because there are

上端神桥东侧（局部）／上图
East Side of Upper Spirit Bridge (Partial) / Upper
上端神桥西侧（局部）／下图
West Side of Upper Spirit Bridge (Partial) / Lower
上端神桥神路／右图
Spirit Path of Upper Spirit Bridge / Right

natural waters under the bridges inside Shanhai Pass, but there are only artificial waters outside the Pass. Spirit Bridge of Fuling Imperial Tomb is built inside Red Gate while that of Zhaoling Imperial Tomb is built outside Red Gate. For a long time, I had thought there wasn't spirit bridge in Yong Mausoleum, but later I found the inconspicuous bridge near the first barrier gate on a narrow ditch over one chi (Chinese traditional unit of length, equal to 1/3 meter). However, why the bridge inside Zhaoling Imperial Tomb was designed flat remains a riddle to me.

Spirit Bridge, as its name implies, is a bridge built on Spirit Path. There are two spirit bridges in Fuling Imperial Tomb; of which one is dry bridge, used only for drainage. Spirit Bridge is one architectural form commonly used in the mausoleums of Qing Dynasty. It can be used both for decoration of mausoleums and practical purposes. Spirit Bridge is used to protect mausoleums from being eroded by rain. Inside a mausoleum, there are some man-made or natural drainage ditches, also called "Dragon Beard Ditch." Spirit Bridge is a drainage tunnel on Spirit Path. Before, when it came to rainy season, the water converged, and ran out from east to west. Seen from afar, it looks like a waterfall suspended in the sky and a silvery ribbon as the topography of Spirit Bridge is at a higher elevation, which is spectacular as one famous scene.

一百单八蹬上铺设成品字形的石砖 / 右页图
Stone bricks of 108 Steps paved in 品 -shape / Right Page

[108 蹬墙宽0.3米，内宽5.85米，长35.46米。两边砖各宽0.2米。至神桥砖0.8米]
(108 Steps is 5.85 meters wide and 35.46 meters long with its side walls 0.3 meter wide. Bricks of the two side walls are all 0.2 meter wide, and the ones of Spirit Bridge are 0.8 meter wide)

清陵独一的一百单八蹬

关于神道的设置，清代陵寝中还有一项特殊规定，就是在神道与隆恩门之间必须修一座建筑做隔断，名曰"一眼望不断"，寓意大清江山万世一系，绵延不断。为此，有的清陵在神道上修龙凤门，昭陵中则修建了神功圣德碑。福陵中不仅建有神功圣德碑，而且根据地理条件，巧妙地依山势建了"福陵天蹬"，俗称"一百零八蹬"，起到双重隔断作用，两边还有边墙。有诗云，"欲知福陵绝佳处，石阶送尔上天登"，福陵天蹬是清皇陵中独一无二的建筑形式，永陵和昭陵都没有一百单八蹬，关内清陵寝中也没有这样的建筑。而它的来源有两种说法，一种是与星宿有关，天上有三十六天罡星和七十二地煞星，把它们踩在脚底，寓意就是让它们保护福陵。而关于108这个特殊数字的这种用法，我们最熟悉的就是《水浒传》（注解11）里的有一百单八将。数字108还有一种说法就是和佛教有关，佛教认为人一生中的烦恼共有108种，所以必须念108遍经，有108颗念珠，敲108下钟才可消除，所以佛教的很多事情都和108都有关。而在中国，只有两个地方有108蹬，一个是清福陵，另一个就是山西五台山。五台山的108蹬，就是取佛教的说法，因此五台山位列我国佛教四大名山之首。后来的中山陵有392级台阶，但并没有什么特别的含义，我想这也可能是效仿福陵中的一百单八蹬建的。与努尔哈赤同时代的日本将军德川家康的墓在山上台阶也比清福陵的多，但是都没有福陵这么多寓意在里面。

BEST PLACE OF FULING IMPERIAL TOMB-108 STEPS

On setup of Spirit Path, it was regulated that a partition has to be built between Spirit Path and Eminent Favor Hall in Qing mausoleums, which is called "Endless View," signifying eternity of Qing Dynasty. Dragon-phoenix Gates were built on Spirit Path in some mausoleums, and Stele Pavilion of Divine Merits was set up in Zhaoling Imperial Tomb while besides Stele Pavilion of Divine Merits, following its topography, Heaven Steps were built in Fuling Imperial Tomb, also called "108 Steps," serving dual partition function, and along either side of the Steps are there two side walls. "If you want to have the best sight of Fuling Imperial Tomb, the stone steps will lead you to Heaven." The architectural form of Heaven Steps is unparalleled in the mausoleums of Qing Dynasty, among which there is no such Steps in Yong and Zhaoling Imperial Tombs. There is no Heavens Steps in Qing mausoleums inside the Pass, either. It originates from two versions of stories: one is related to constellation, as there are 36 big dippers and 72 malignant stars in the heaven. Treading them under feet signifies they are held there to protect Fuling Imperial Tomb forever; the other is that the use of the particular number 108 comes from the novel Water Margins we are most familiar with, in which there are 108 generals. The number 108 is related to Buddhism, as the Buddhism holds the idea that there are 108 types of irritations in one's life, therefore, you must recite Buddhist Scriptures 108 times, hold 108 prayer beads, and beat the bell 108 times before you get rid of these irritations. Buddha has a lot of things related to 108. In China, there are two places that have "108 Steps", one of which is Fuling Imperial Tomb, the other of which is Mountain Wutai of Shanxi Province. The 108 steps in Mountain Wutai adopt the Buddhist's idea, as it is the leader of the five famous mountains of Buddhism. There are 392 steps in Zhongshan Mausoleum, but there isn't special meaning implied, which might follow the suit of Fuling Imperial Tomb. There are more steps on the tomb hill of Japanese General Tokugawa Ieyasu, who was in the same time of Nurhaci, but there is not so much connotation.

神功圣德碑楼／下图、右页图
Stele Pavilion of Divine Merits / Lower, Right Page
[长15.47米，宽15.47米，高13.35米]
(15.47 meters long, 15.47 meters wide, 13.35 meters high)

退役的神龟

大碑楼，建于康熙二十七年（1688年），碑上用满、汉两种文字合璧详细地记载了努尔哈赤的生平，为大清国创业的艰辛以及丰功伟绩。碑楼底部为须弥座式台基，碑楼呈正方形，九脊重檐歇山式，飞檐斗栱，四面各开单券拱门，四周青砖墁地，俗称"海墁"。碑楼朝南一面的海墁上，两侧各有一龙首，俯伏在地面上，龙口上颚张开。清代嘉庆九年维修福陵档案中，有"海墁散水"记载，足见两个龙口为福陵地宫的排水管道出口。碑楼内矗立着将近7米，重达50吨的神功圣德碑，由一个鳌身龙首的神兽所伏，是用一整块岩石雕刻而成，石碑最下面布满海水江崖纹饰，四角各雕鱼、鳖、虾、蟹于漩涡的基础部分，为"地袱"，每到阴雨天，漩涡内会蓄满水，其实这就是古称"月晕而风，础润而雨"的现象。地袱上为驮碑的赑屃（注解12），碑头由6条蛟龙盘绕，正面是康熙皇帝亲笔的"大清福陵神功圣德碑"，碑文落款为"孝曾孙嗣皇帝玄烨"。

相传皇太极在初建福陵时，沿袭中原建造皇陵的规矩，为努尔哈赤在陵区内建立了"神功圣德碑"。由于对汉文化的了解不足，还发生了一点小误会，他们把驮石碑的"龙王"之子雕刻成乌龟。当康熙皇帝东巡祭祖时发现这一错误，立即命其更换，结果，原来驮碑的乌龟就此退役，后来被遗弃在西红墙外。不过正是因为有了神龟流泪，我们才能清晰地认识，满汉两族文化的融合，是一个漫长而渐进的过程，而被遗弃的神龟则成了这一历史进程的最好见证者。传说，每到阴天下雨之时，石龟的眼睛里就会流出伤感的泪水，这就是著名的神龟流泪的传说。

我想，神龟可能是感到委屈了吧，同是福陵的守护者，石象生都还在，还给加了汉白玉底座，却单单把自己给挪出来了。由此，我想到一个典故，同一块石头，一半被刻成了佛像，一半则被刻成佛脚下的踏石，踏石心理不平衡，问被刻成佛像的石头，"为什么人们都踩着我，却朝拜你？"佛像回答："我可是经过了人们的千刀万剐，而你只有六刀。"神龟流泪和石象生一样，都是石头，只是一块被刻成了驮碑的乌龟，一块被刻成了站班的石象生。其实，当初人们朝拜的也不是神龟，而是神龟背上驮着的碑上的皇帝名号。无论是神碑也好，神龟也好，石象生也好，同样是石头，只是放的位置不同，地位才截然不同，终归不过就是块石头。

由此，我又想人生不一定都如军人一样退伍退役，实际上每个人都有退休的时候，在一个岗位上辛苦了一辈子，忽然有一天清闲了，难免有些失落。这也是人以自己的角度去揣度神龟的心情吧，可能它也渴望重新回到陵寝内，继续坚守自己的岗位，所以终日头都望着陵寝的方向。不过，虽然神龟不在陵内了，也没有闲着，今天它已经是一个景点，经常有人特意前来朝拜它，甚至还编成了"摸摸神龟头，总也不发愁，摸摸神龟尾……"这样的吉祥语。如果真要说遗忘，那么在方城西南角的帐篷石的命运，可能才是最可怜的吧。

我曾多次想拍到神龟流泪的情景，晴天也去拍，下雨天也跑去拍，可惜，多年都不能如愿。虽然神龟一直没能拍好，但是在拍摄过程中我悟出了人生的一些道理……

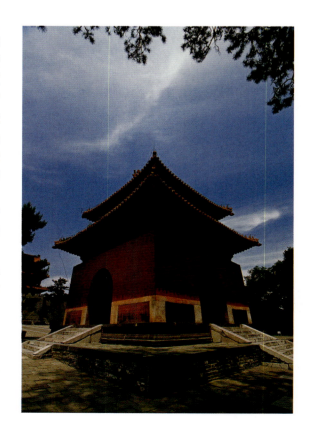

RETIRED DIVINE TURTLE

Great Stele Pavilion of Divine Merits was built in the 27th ruling year of Emperor Kangxi (1688), on which the caption records in Manchu and Chinese the lifetime of Nurhaci in detail, the arduousness he had undergone and his great feats he had achieved. Foundation of the stele pavilion is of Sumeru-throne base, and the pavilion is squarely shaped with hip-and-gable roof of nine-ridged purlin and double eaves. Archways are set around its four sides and its ground is paved with grey bricks, which is called "Hai Man" (Large Pavement). Upon Large Pavement in the south-facing pavilion, there is a dragon head on each side, bending over the ground with its upper jaw wide open. In the maintenance record of Fuling Imperial Tomb in the 9th year of Emperor Jiaqing, there is a record of "Large Pavement Water Dispersing," where you can see the dragon mouths are exits of the drainage pipes of Fuling Imperial Tomb. Inside the stele pavilion, there is Stele of Divine Merits, seven meters high weighing 50 tons. It is carried by a holy animal with dragon head and turtle body, carved from an entire rock. The underneath of the Stele Pavilion is covered with Seawater Hill designs. The four corners are carved with patterns of fish, turtle, shrimp and crab, which are called "ground cloth wrapper." On rainy days, the whirlpool will store up water, which was described in ancient times as "a halo around the moon indicates the rising of wind; the damp on a plinth signifies approaching rain." Over the ground cloth wrapper, there is a giant Bixi (Note 12) carrying a tablet. The head of the Stele is entwined with six winding flood dragons. On its facade is the handwriting of Emperor Kangxi "Stele of Divine Merits of Fuling Imperial Tomb of Great Qing." The subscription of the Stele is "Filial Great-grand Son Emperor Xuan Ye."

It is said that at the beginning of its construction, Emperor Hong Taiji followed the custom of Central Plain and built Great Stele Pavilion of Divine Merits inside the mausoleum area for Nurhaci. Due to insufficient knowledge of Han culture, there had been a misunderstanding. They carved the son of "Dragon King" carrying the stone tablet into a turtle. During the ancestral worship tour of Emperor Kang Xi, he discovered the mistake and ordered to have it changed. The original turtle carrying the tablet was abandoned to the outside of West Red Gate. It can be seen that the integration of Manchu culture and Han culture is a long and gradual process, and the abandoned turtle is the best evidence. On rainy days, the stone turtle is full of heartbroken tears, which forms a famous legendary scene "Tear-shedding Turtle."

I think the turtle might feel wronged; it must wonder that as protectors of the Mausoleum, why the other stone statues are still standing there, and marble bases are added, but only I am removed out of the Mausoleum? They are all there, even supplied with white marble bases, not to mention my hard work for shouldering the heavy stone tablet. This reminds me of a story that a stone carved into two halves, with one half as Buddha statue, and the other half as the stepping stone of the Buddha foot; the stepping stone is mentally unbalanced, asking statue stone, "why do people all step on me, but worship you?" and the statue replies, "I am carved hundreds of times, and you only have six cuts." Just like the stone statues, the tear-shedding turtle is carved into a stone turtle shouldering a stone tablet, and the other one is carved into the stone statue standing on guard. In fact, people didn't worship the turtle, but Emperor's name on the monument upon the turtle. Just because the monument, turtle, and statue are located in the different places, their statues are different; after all, they are all stones.

Thus, I think that people can not always retire as servicemen do, but in fact, everyone has to retire; after a lifetime of hard work on a certain position, a sudden retirement might cause a sense of loss. People might be just conjecturing the mood of the tear-shedding turtle: it may also be eager to return to the Mausoleum, sticking to its own post, so it keeps heading towards the Mausoleum all day long. However, although the turtle is not in the tomb anymore, it is not idle. Today it already becomes a scenery spot, which many visitors come specifically to worship, and there is even an auspicious saying "to touch the turtle head, worries will fade; to touch the turtle tail ⋯" Talking about being abandoned, fates of tent stones in the southwest corner of Square City might be the most miserable.

I have tried many times to photograph scenes of turtle shedding tears, in sunny days or rainy days; unfortunately, I never succeed. I failed again and again in taking a satisfactory picture of the turtle, but I get to know something about life during the shooting ⋯

Retired Divine Turtle / Left

Stele of Divine Merits / Right Page

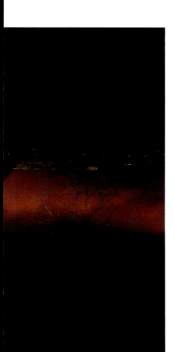

退役的神龟／左页图
Retired Divine Turtle / Left Page
大碑楼／下图
Great Stele Pavilion / Lower

神碑幻影

福陵、昭陵中都各有一座神功圣德碑，而关外三陵中的永陵却有四座神功圣德碑，可以说是碑楼最多的清朝皇陵。纵观清朝历史，功绩最大的皇帝，可能都会想到康熙皇帝。而不仅是我们这样认为，古人也这样认为，所以，圣德神功碑亭内立着双碑以彰显这位皇帝的功劳，从此成为定制。因此，雍正帝、乾隆帝、嘉庆帝的陵寝的神功圣德碑也都是两块，才形成了这样几位皇帝的神功圣德碑都是双碑的特殊情形，直到道光帝，这种情况才有所变化。清代皇帝中道光帝没有立神功圣德碑，因为清朝祖制中规定，"凡后世皇帝失国土尺地寸土者，不得立神功圣德碑"。其实历数各朝各代，清朝是出明君最多的朝代，清12个皇帝，每个都很勤勉，可惜，到了清末，西方列强的发展远远超过了清朝，在强大的铜炮火枪面前，长矛和大刀是根本无法取胜的。

福陵的神功圣德碑有一种奇特的现象，每当阴雨天气，碑身的背面就会隐隐约约显现出人形，身材修颀、头挽高髻、宽袍大袖，如飘飘然踏云而来的观音侧身像，所以又称观音石。这种现象，被称之为神碑幻影。奇怪的是，昭陵里的神功圣德碑竟然也同样有这种奇特的现象。从古至今，"大清神功圣德碑"的这个现象引起诸多文人雅士的观赏兴致，成为清代"留都十景"之一的"神碑幻影"。《陪都纪略》（注解13）还有一首诗赞誉此景说："古石成形瑞气全，胜似丹青巧手镌。两陵（昭陵、福陵）背后生神像，可入陪都志略篇。"道光九年有一位叫何汝霖的大臣随皇帝东巡昭陵祭祖，也因为听说此碑奇特特意在祭陵余暇来此观赏，据他揣摩之后说此种的人形很像"观音大士"，这在《何氏沈阳纪程》（注解14）里可得到证明。《沈阳县志》也称此碑为"神碑"；也有人称之为"美人石"、"观音石"。《沈故》（注解15）里还说，碑的人形象是"汉寿亭侯"诸葛亮。总之，真是仁者见仁、智者见智。而这种碑石显形现象不仅见于神功圣德碑，史书记载，昭陵的大明楼上的圣号碑的背面也会显现人形，而民国军阀冯德麟在担任奉天山陵守护大臣时，还特意派画匠按碑上的纹理涂上颜色，画成一幅"麻姑献寿图"。《沈故》记载，辽南耀州庙有一座石碑能显现出一尊"韦驼神像"。这种现象在全国其他地方也有发现，如四川省仁寿县黑龙滩风景区唐文化遗址处，有两块隐形碑，乍看上去光洁无痕，泼水其上，右侧碑石上，立即显现出一行楷书大字，左侧碑石则显现一幅功力深厚的墨竹图，字和画随水气消尽而复隐。

我推测，福陵神功圣德碑能够呈现人像，主要是由于石碑纹理密度小、并由善于吸收水分的干松石质构成，所以受潮后，碑上部分纹理颜色便变深、纹理突出所致。奇石天然纹理，人看后想象出各种幻影。人，才是最大的幻影题材创造者。而至于两陵的碑都成人像，究竟是巧合，还是故意为之，不得而解。古代建筑至今也仍有很多未解之谜，神功圣德碑算一个吧。

PHANTOMS OF DIVINE STELE

There is a Stele of Divine Merits respectively in Fu and Zhaoling Imperial Tombs. But there are four in Yong Mausoleum, with the most of the three mausoleums. Throughout the history of Qing Dynasty, the emperor with the greatest achievements should be Emperor Kangxi. Not only we think so, but also our ancestors did. So the two steles inside Stele Pavilion of Divine Merits highlight the emperor's divine merits, and since then it became a tradition to set up steles of divine merits. Therefore, there are also two steles of divine merits in the mausoleums of emperors Yongzheng, Qianlong and Jiaqing, but from Emperor Daoguang, this tradition began to change. No stele of divine merits was set up for Emperor Daoguang, as it was regulated in the ancient system of Qing Dynasty, "Any future emperor shall not deserve steles of divine merits if he loses one inch of land." Actually, there are 12 emperors in Qing Dynasty, which is a dynasty full of the most sagacious emperors, and all of the emperors were assiduous. Pitifully, at the end of Qing Dynasty, the western powers surpassed Qing Dynasty with a large gap. Compared with cannons and muskets, there wasn't any chance for spears and broadswords to win.

There is a special phenomenon about Stele of Divine Merits in Fuling Imperial Tomb. On cloudy or rainy days, the back of the tablet will have a vague figure resembling Guanyin (Buddhist goddess) treading the cloud, wearing a hair tie, broad sleeves and loose robe, which is also called Kuanyin (goddess of mercy) Stone. This phenomenon is called Phantom of Divine Stele. Strangely, there is similar magic phenomenon in Zhaoling Imperial Tomb. From the ancient times to now, "Stele of Divine Merits of Great Qing" has aroused interests of many scholars and bachelors. The so-called "Phantom of Divine Stele" became one of the ten scenic spots in this old capital of Qing Dynasty. There is a poem in Memoirs of Shengjing (Note 13) praising the scene: "Ancient stone is carved with auspicious bearing, resembling a supreme drawing by skilful hand. Pictures of Kuan Yin are generated in two mausoleums, which can be recorded in memoirs of Shengjing ..." In the 9th year of Emperor Daoguang, a minister named He Rulin followed Emperor travelling eastwards to Zhaoling Imperial Tomb for ancestral worship. On hearing that the tablet was unique, he paid a special visit in his spare time. It is said that he figured out what Buddhist goddess Kuan Yin was like, which was recorded in Travel Notes to Shenyang (Note 14). Shenyang County Annals records this tablet as "Divine Stele." Some others also call it "Beauty Stone", "Kuan Yin Stone". According to Shengu (Note 15), figure of the tablet is like Zhu Geliang, Marquis of Han Shou. In one word, "the benevolent see benevolence and the wise see wisdom." This type of phantom is not only limited to Stele of Divine Merits. According to historical records, there is a human figure on back of the title tablet of Soul-tower in Zhaoling Imperial Tomb, while Feng Delin, the national warlord had painted a picture of Mago Offering Birthday Gifts according to the design of the figure on the tablet by coloring it when he acted as the defense minister of Mukden Mausoleum. It is recorded in Shengu that Yaozhou Temple of Liaonan has a "Weituo Buddha Statue". Similar phenomena are discovered in other places of China, too. In cultural heritage site of Tang Dynasty, Heilongtan Scenic Spot of Renshou County, Sichuan Province, there are two tablets, which you can see nothing on your first sight. But after sprinkling water on it, a line of regular script characters emerge on the right tablet while a black bamboo painting on the left. The characters and painting disappear with disappearance of steam.

I infer that Stele of Divine Merits in Fuling Imperial Tomb can reflect the human figure, mainly because texture of the stele is loose, which is composed of dry loose sandstones, and good at absorbing water. After humidified, color of the tablet texture becomes intensified and clearer, therefore the figure appears. People fantasize after viewing the figure. Actually, people are phantom makers. Why figures of the stones in two mausoleums all resemble human? Nobody knows whether it is a coincidence or a predetermined design. There are a lot of perplexities in ancient architecture, and Stele of Divine Merits is one among them.

清东陵（景陵）神功圣德双碑 / 下一图
Double Stele Pavilion of Divine Merits of East Qing Mausoleum (Jing Mausoleum) / Lower First

废弃的帐篷石 / 下二图
Abandoned Tent Stone / Lower Second

退役的神龟 / 右页图
Retired Divine Turtle / Right Page

饽饽房、齐班房遗址／左图
Relics of Bo Bo Fang (Pastry House) and Qi Ban Fang (Tomb Guards House) / Left
清东陵（孝陵）祭祀隆恩殿内陈设／上图
Sacrificial Offerings inside Eminent Favor Hall in East Qing Mausoleum (Xiao Mausoleum) / Upper

福陵祭祀

碑楼两边，东侧原有回廊式茶房、膳房，西侧有果房、饽饽房、涤器房、齐班房，均为三间，分别是制作祭品、贮藏祭品以及官员侯祭的地方。现在"饽饽房"和"齐班房"都仅存遗址，申遗以后用玻璃罩保护起来了。夏天时，玻璃罩周围长满青草，远远看去，玻璃罩像一个花棚，需工人爬进去锄草。不仅不利于观看，玻璃罩里面的温度对遗址的保护也是非常不科学的。所以我想，这种保护方法真是值得商榷的。事实上，饽饽房只是用于蒸饽饽的地方，祭祀摆设和供品是在隆恩殿及东西配殿。

清朝入关以后，由于受汉族文化及生活习俗的影响，满族的文化和生活形式也发生了变化，这些变化也反映在陵寝的祭祀上。陵寝的祭祀一直到乾隆初年才完全固定下来。一般祭祀前，要经过大量的准备工作，这些准备工作就需用到碑楼两侧那些看似不重要，其实最具实用价值的建筑群。

一般，大祭的准备工作繁重复杂，福陵祭祀由盛京礼部主管，福陵的掌关防衙门负责具体承办，盛京将军衙门、盛京内务在、工部、户部、刑部、兵部、奉天府、太常寺（掌管祭祀的衙门）等衙门也要全力协作，参与祭祀。具体而言，准备工作主要有，备办祭品，祭器，供品等。祭祀所用的祭器极为贵重精美，有金、银、铜器等贵金属器具，还有珐琅器、瓷器等，特别是金银器上还镶嵌有各种价值连城的宝石。供品，要求毛色纯黑，头角端正的乌牛一头，羊两只，做"整牛供"（注解16）和"整羊献"。满汉风味俱全，除山珍海味、飞禽走兽外，还有酒、奶制品，如奶茶及萨其马等。所有供品，都是满族祖先最喜欢食用的。祭品数量的多少，视墓主人的地位高低而定。地位，封号虽然相同，但与皇帝的关系密切程度不同，葬位不同，其祭祀形式，祭品数量也有差异。季节的不同，也会使祭品发生变化。尽管多有变化，但有一个基本的标准。总的来说，祭品分两大类，一是膳品，一是饽饽。

饽饽中又分饽饽和果品两种。所有这些，都耗资惊人，是平常百姓想都不敢想的。而准备工作也是很早就开始了，因为供品量之巨大，不是一天两天就能够准备充足的。

此外，还有送祝版、佛花。祝版一般被供奉在特制的龙亭里，龙亭类似于一顶亭子式的小轿，祭陵前请祝版时，盛京兵部的十名官员要随行恭送到福陵的东配殿。一路上，龙亭前设两个手持木棍的引路人，所到之处行人必须回避，躲避不及可面墙而立，否则就会受到引路人木棍的击打。而清明大祭时，盛京礼部还要备办一份佛花送往福陵。佛花又叫佛堂花，上面有用彩纸、金箔、银箔等扎成的龙、凤以及各种花卉。大祭时，此花供于隆恩殿的供案之上，祭陵毕，将其挪至大殿一角，直到岁暮祭陵完毕时焚化。此外，还要准备敷土用具等。各种准备工作就绪，祭陵仪式也就可以开始了。

清陵祭祀不仅礼节繁缛，而且等级极为森严，但这只不过是福陵例行的常规祭祀，因为同祭一陵，主祭者地位不同也会导致礼仪各异，上述种种福陵祭礼的主祭者还并不是清朝的最高统治者，而每当皇帝亲临，场面就更加盛大了。因为盛京是清朝的开国都城，既是龙兴之地，又为祖宗陵寝之所在，因而清帝在入主中原后，对这一祖宗发祥重地给予了特殊的关注。自康熙十年(1671年)始，圣祖康熙继承父志来到盛京，祭祀了坐落在盛京的祖宗陵寝，福陵是他祭祀的第一座祖陵，从而开创了清帝"东巡祭祖"的定制，在此后的150年间，清朝皇帝接连不断地亲自谒陵，从康熙到光绪这八位皇帝，共亲谒祖陵209次，其中盛京三陵10次，东陵125次，西陵74次。谒陵次数最多的当属乾隆皇帝，仅在位期间就谒陵69次。由皇帝亲自主持举行隆重的祭祀大典，成为福陵历史上无以复加的盛事。

历朝皇家都把上陵礼，皇陵祭祀作为推崇皇权，维护统治的一种重要形式和手段，他们提出"圣天子孝先天下，首重山陵"。这里所说的"重山陵"，不仅指的是山陵的营建，更主要的是指对山陵祭祀的重视。和所有朝代帝王一样，清代同样信奉"事死如事生，事亡如事存"的理念。关于清代陵寝的祭祀礼仪，在定鼎中原日益汉化的基础上，既仿明制依汉俗，又结合本民族的风俗特点，有着一整套系统而完备的祭祀制度。清朝皇帝对陵寝的重视超过了往代，因此也可以说清朝的陵寝祭祀已经形成了一种文化现象，并达到了顶峰。

清朝按祭祀种类规模大致可分为大祭、小祭和特祭。福陵大祭包括每年的清明、中元(七月十五)、冬至、岁暮(除夕)。福陵忌辰大祭每年举行两次，太祖的忌日和孝慈高皇后的忌日；其中，清明、中元、冬至、岁暮又称"四时大祭"，是祭祀中等级最高、礼制最繁琐、祭品最丰盛的祭祀形式。另外，清明大祭中最有特色的是"敷土礼"，即是往宝顶上添土，这与民间培土修坟的习俗相似。乾隆二年(1737年)前，敷土礼相当繁琐，每次要敷土十三担，承祭官、总管、掌关防官等十三人同时登上宝顶添土。乾隆继位后对这项制度做了改变，因为他觉得这么多人登上皇陵宝顶，有失对祖宗的敬重，于是发圣旨说："清明山陡增土十三担，向沿前明旧制、并无取义似觉太烦。今拟各陵增上一担，俱令承祭官跪上土于宝顶。庶践履不至多人，益用诚敬。"

小祭，又叫"常祭""朔望祭"，包括每月的朔望即初一、十五；小祭比大祭无论就祭祀规模还是承祭官的品级等方面都低。首先，祭礼时不请神牌，只打开神龛的门和幔帐，对神龛而祭。祭品也不像大祭那样丰盛。其次，承祭官也不劳宗室将军等人大驾，仅由福陵关防衙门的掌关防官主祭。参加祭礼的人数也比大祭少得多，与民间给神佛烧香上供的做法类似。

除以上祭祀外，还包括特祭，就是指因国家大典而在福陵临时举行的告祭礼，如每年皇帝或皇太后生日举行的"万寿告祭"，为皇太后加徽号举行的告祭，或出征凯旋向陵告祭，或皇子每隔三年来此行礼，此外还有途经盛京的官员或者到盛京上任的新官也要到福陵拜谒。不得不感叹，清代如此频繁的祭祀，且每次祭祀祭品丰奢，仪式盛大，难免损耗国力。然而，对于帝王来说，这些却都是值得的。因为祭祖，这样的仪式，如此兴师动众，其实并不是真正为了故去的先祖，而是做给世人看的，为了威慑天下。

涤器房／左页图·下图
Cleaning House/ Left Page, Lower
[长15.75米，宽17.35米，高9.14米]
(15.75 meters ong, 17.65 meters wide, 9.14 meters high)

FULING IMPERIAL TOMB SACRIFICE

On both sides of the Stele Pavilion, there were cloister-style tea and food house on the east side, and fruit house, pastry house, cleaning house and tomb guards house on the west side; there were both three houses, used respectively for making sacrificial offerings, storing offerings as well as resting of officials. Now, there remain only the ruins of pastry house and rest house, being protected with glass shades after application for List of World Heritage. In summer, grassy glass shade looks like a flower trellis from afar. It is not conducive to view, and temperature inside glass shades is unscientific for protection of the ruins. So I think, this kind of protection is really questionable. In fact, the pastry house is used to prepare steam breads. The sacrificial articles and offerings are prepared and displayed in Eminent Favor Hall East and its West Side-halls.

After Qing's entry at Shanhai Pass, their culture and life style of Manchu had changed due to the influence of Han culture and customs, which were also reflected in the sacrifices of Mausoleums. The mausoleum sacrifices are not completely fixed until the early ruling years of Emperor Qianlong. Generally speaking, there is a lot of preparatory work to engage in prior to the sacrifice, which requires the use of those seemingly unimportant but actually most practical buildings on both sides of the Stele Pavilion.

Generally, the preparatory work of grand sacrifice is tiresome and complex, which is superintended by Shengjing Board of Rites and Ceremonies, and specifically catered by Frontier Defense Yamen of Fuling Imperial Tomb, and Shengjing General Yamen, Shengjing Imperial Household Department, Board of Works, Board of Revenue, Board of Punishments, Board of War, Mukden City Hall and Taichang Temple (Yamen in charge of sacrifices) have to fully cooperate and participate in the sacrifice. In particular, the preparatory work includes preparing sacrifices, sacrificial utensils, offerings and so on. Very expensive and fine are these sacrificial utensils used for the ceremony, which are precious metal utensils such as gold, silver and copper, as well as enamel, and porcelain utensils, especially gold and silver utensils mounted all kinds of priceless gems. The offerings are required to be one black cattle and two sheep with absolutely black fur, proper heads and horns for "Entire Cattle Sacrifice" (Note 16) and "Entire Sheep Sacrifice." There are both Manchu and Han flavors, and in addition to delicacies of birds and beasts, there are also wines, dairy products such as milk and candied fritter. All offerings are favorite food of Manchu ancestors. Quantity of the sacrifice is depending on social statues of the tomb owner. Even with the same statues and title, different levels of closeness to Emperor and different buried locations adopt different sacrificial forms and different numbers of offerings. Offerings also vary with seasons. Whatever the difference is, there is a basic standard. Overall, offerings may be divided into two categories: meal and pastry, and the latter could be divided into pastry and fruit. All of these are too costly for ordinary people to imagine. The preparatory work begins very early, for such huge amount of offerings could not be done in one or two days.

In addition, there are rituals of sending Prayer Tablets and Buddhist flowers. Prayer Tablets are generally enshrined in a customized dragon pavilion, which is similar to a pavilion-style sedan chair; ten officials of Shengjing Board of War should escort Prayer Tablets to its east side hall prior to the sacrifice. Along the way, there are two guides with sticks in front of the dragon pavilion, and pedestrians on the road must step aside; and if there is no time to step aside, they have to face the wall standing; otherwise they will be striken by guides with their sticks. In the grand sacrifice of Qingming Festival (also Tomb-sweeping Festival), Shengjing Board of Rites and Ceremonies also has to prepare Buddhist flowers to Fuling Imperial Tomb. Buddhist flowers are also known as Buddhist temple flowers with dragons, phoenixes and a variety of flowers on color paper, gold foil and silver foil. On such occasions, these flowers are enshrined on the altar table of Eminent Favor Hall, and then are moved to the corner of the hall after the sacrifice and incinerated till the completion of the close-year sacrifice. Besides, the hilling-up tools shall be prepared. When all preparatory work is done, the sacrificial ritual will be started.

The sacrifices in Qing Dynasty are not only in complex etiquette, but also in strict hierarchy. The above-mentioned is only routine practices in Fuling Imperial Tomb, because different statuses of the ceremony officiant will lead to different rites even in the same mausoleum. The above mentioned officiant in Fuling Imperial Tomb is not supreme ruler of Qing Dynasty, and if Emperor presents in person, the sacrificial scene will be even more magnificent. For Shengjing is the founding capital of Qing Dynasty and cemetery of their ancestors, Qing emperors all pay their special attention to this cradle land of their ancestors after entry to Central Plains. In the 10th year of Emperor Kangxi (1671), following his

清东陵（景陵）班房／左上图
Ban Fang (Tomb Guards House) in East Qing Mausoleum (Jing Mausoleum) / Upper Left
果房／左下图
Furit House / Lower Left
清东陵（景陵）饽饽房烟筒／右图
Chimney of Bo Bo Fang (Pastry House) in East Qing Mausoleum (Jing Mausoleum) / Fight

father's footsteps, Kangxi came to Shengjing to offer sacrifices to their ancestral mausoleum. Fuling Imperial Tomb is the first ancestral cemetery that he had ever worshiped, thus creating the custom of Qing emperors, "East Tour for Ancestor Worship"; in the next century and a half, Qing emperors kept doing this personally. From Kangxi to Guangxu, there are 8 emperors who made totally 209 times worship, of which 10 times for Three Mausoleums in Shengjing, 125 times for East Mausoleum and 74 times for West Mausoleum. The emperor who worshiped most frequently is undoubtedly Qianlong, who had done for 69 times during his reign. The sacrificial ceremony held by Emperor himself is the most magnificent event in the history of Fuling Imperial Tomb.

Royal families of every dynasty regard sacrificial worship in the royal mausoleums as the most important form and means to value their imperial powers and maintain their reign. They put forward the idea that "wise emperors are more filial than the rest of his people, so they firstly value their mausoleums." As to "value their mausoleums," it not only refers to the construction of mausoleum, but primarily to their attention to mausoleum sacrifices. Like all other dynasties, Qing Dynasty believes in the concept of "Honoring the dead as the living." Mausoleums of Qing Dynasty and their sacrificial ceremonies have accumulated a whole set of mature systems with features of both Han customs and their own ethnic rites, which are based on foundation of their regime in Central Plains. The importance that Qing emperors attach to mausoleums surpassed the former dynasties, and therefore it can be said that mausoleum rituals of Qing Dynasty have reached their peak as a cultural phenomenon.

According to sacrificial scale of Qing Dynasty, it can be divided into grand, small and special. Grand sacrifices of Fuling Imperial Tomb include Qingming Festival, Ghost Festival (Lunar July 15), Winter Solstice, close of the year (Lunar New Year's Eve) and sacrifices of death day; sacrifices of death day are held twice a year, including anniversary of death days of Hong Taiji and Queen Xiaocigao, among which Qingming Festival, Ghost Festival, Winter Solstice, close of the year are also known as "Grand sacrifices in four seasons" with the highest level, the most complicated rites and most sumptuous offerings in all the sacrifices. In addition, "Hilling-up Rite" is the most featured grand sacrifice in Qingming Festival, which is to add soil on top of the grave, similar to the civil custom of tomb reheaping. Before the 2nd (1737)

ruling year of Emperor Qianlong, the Hilling-up rite was rather cumbersome, 13 dan (ancient Chinese unit of weight, equivalent to 50 kilograms) of soil must be hilled up by 13 people such as host officer, manger and Frontier Defense officer at the same time on top of the grave. Emperor Qianlong changed this regulation after his enthronement, because he thought that it is disrespectful to ancestors that so many people step on top of the grave; he then issued an imperial edict:

"Adding 13 dan onto the hill in Qingming Festival is to continue the old system of Ming Dynasty, which seems meaningless and complicated. Now we require the host officer to knee down and add 1 dan onto the hill. Respect and sincerity are more important than the number of officers."

Small-size sacrifice, also called "Regular sacrifice" or "Lunar sacrifice," much smaller than Grand sacrifice in terms of size and lower in rank of host officer, took place on the 1st day and 15th day of each month. Firstly, the divine memorial tablet will not be engaged in the sacrifice, in which people simply open the gate and curtains of shrine and worship towards it. The offerings are not as luxurious as in grand sacrifice. Secondly, the host officer could be Frontier Defense officer in Frontier Defense Yamen of Fuling Imperial Tomb instead of a royal family member or General. The number of participants is much smaller than that in grand sacrifice, which is quite similar to civilian practice of sacrifices.

In addition to the above sacrifices, there is special sacrifice, which is a temporal rite due to national ceremonies held in Fuling Imperial Tomb, such as "Boundless Longevity Announcement Sacrifice" for birthdays of Emperor or Empress dowager, Announcement Sacrifice awarding emblems for Empress dowager, Announcement Sacrifice before and after a war, or courtesy paid by princes every three years. Moreover, all the officials passing by Mukden or new officials of Mukden need to pay tribute to Fuling Imperial Tomb. We have to say that these complex sacrificial rituals, strict ranks, luxurious offerings will cost a lot and inevitably damage national power. However, for Emperor, these are worth doing, because the rituals such as ancestral worship are not really held for the deceased, but for deterring his people under reign

果房／左页图
Fruit House / Left Page
[长16.36米, 宽19.3米, 高8.8米]
(16.36 meters long, 19.3 meters wide, 8.8 meters high)
果房冬景与秋景／左上图、右上图
Winter and Autumn Scenery of Fruit House / Upper Left, Upper Right
隆恩殿内祭品陈设／下图
Sacrificial Offerings Inside Eminent Favor Hall / Lower

方城／上图、右图 Square City / Upper, Right
[高约5米，周长370米](It is about 5 meters high, with a perimeter of 370 meters)
神功圣德碑楼前的吐水残"龙"／下图
Relic of "Dragon" (for Drainage) in Front of Stele Pavilion of Divine Merits / Lower

清代帝陵独有的方城

在大碑楼北面，有一个城堡式建筑，叫做方城，这也是福陵的主要部分，也是陵园的祭祀建筑区，更是最具满族特色的建筑区。方城东、西、南城上的雉堞（注解17），实际上是守城人向外射箭的地方。城上有4米多宽的马道，路面微微倾斜，有排水的功效，令人不得不慨叹古人设计智慧之高明。方城上还有楼梯蹬，可以直接从外面直接登上方城马道，而关内的清帝陵则一般都是内置楼梯。方城内包括陵寝的核心建筑隆恩殿及东西配殿等。

方城，一直困惑着我，它既不是最大的城，也不是最小的城，如沈阳都可以叫十里方城，最小的城是北京故宫与北海之间的团城，周长276米，面积4553平方米，福陵方城规模比团城大，比一般的城还小。这让我联想到故宫，沈阳故宫的台上五宫，既然古人讲究"事死如事生"，那么方城是不是仿故宫建的，或者说就是故宫的缩影？由此，我又想到赫图阿拉，赫图阿拉就是建在天然的台上的，而故宫则是建在人工台上。那么皇太极在给努尔哈赤修建陵寝时，很可能是仿造了自己的住所为之修建了福陵。如此一来，福陵方城类似一个城堡就讲得通了。这也是古代帝王希望灵魂永生，在地下依然可以帝业永存的一种表达方式吧。

清代陵寝，关内陵寝一般都没有方城，道光帝的慕陵甚至没有宝城，关外三陵相比，永陵，没有方城，只有很矮的墙，福陵与昭陵类似，福陵方城内有三处大型建筑。尽管孝陵也有一处与关外清陵同名为方城的建筑，却是同名不同概念，关外的方城是相对于月牙城而言的，不是单指形状上是方的就叫方城的，关外的方城都是类似真正的城，里面包含隆恩殿、东西配殿等大型建筑，孝陵的方城却是类似于关外月牙城部分，里面只包含影壁墙和登城台阶，没有实质性建筑，两者除了名字一样，几乎在形制与功能上完全不同。可以说，方城是关外清陵独有的，也是清代帝王陵寝独有的建筑。

隆恩门 / 左图 Eminent Favor Gate / Left
[长 15.62 米, 宽 12.6 米, 高 20.93 米](15.62 meters long, 12.6 meters wide, 20.93 meters high)
东侧宝城城墙 / 上图
East-side Wall of Burial Bastion / Upper
[城高约 5 米, 周长 370 米](Square City is about 5 meters high, with a perimeter of 370 meters)

SQUARE CITY, A UNIQUE BUILDING OF QING MAUSOLEUMS

There is a castle-like building called Square City to the north of Great Stele Pavilion, which is the main part of Fuling Imperial Tomb, the worship building area of the mausoleum and the most distinctive Manchu building area. There are Zhidies (Note 17), the actual battlements on the east, west, south ramparts, from which defenders shoot arrows. On city walls, there is a 4-meter wide riding track, with a road tilting slightly inward, which functions as drainage. I can't help admiring wisdom of ancient people. In addition, there are stairs on Square City, which directly lead to the horse tracks of the City from outside the City. The mausoleums of Qing Dynasty inside the Pass are generally equipped with built-in stairs for access from inside. Inside Square City are main buildings of the Mausoleum such as Eminent Favor Hall and west and east Side-halls.

It always confuses me why Square City can be used to refer to either the biggest or the smallest. For example, Shenyang could also be called Ten-mile Square City, while the smallest city, Tuan City between Forbidden City and North Sea in Beijing is just 276 meters in perimeter, 4,553 square meters in area, with a scale smaller than Fuling Imperial Tomb's Square City. This reminds me of Shenyang Imperial Palace and its five palaces. Since ancient people believe in "Honoring the dead as the living," can we say that Square City is built following this Palace or that it is the very miniature of the Palace? As a result, I think of Early Qing, in which their palace is built on a natural platform. But Shenyang Palace is built on an artificial platform. So when Hong Taiji built a mausoleum for Nurhaci, it is probable that he copied his own residence to construct Fuling Imperial Tomb. Therefore, it makes sense that Fuling Imperial Tomb's Square City looks like a castle, showing that ancient emperors wish their eternal souls could rule the world forever under the ground.

Generally speaking, there are no Square Cities among Qing mausoleums inside Shanhai Pass. For example, there isn't even Burial Bastion inside Mu Mausoleum of Emperor Daoguang. Among Three Mausoleums outside the Shanhai Pass, there are three buildings in Fuling Imperial Tomb as in Zhaoling Imperial Tomb, but there is no square city in Yong Mausoleum except low walls there. Although there is a Square City inside Xiao Mausoleum, but this Square City is different from those outside Shanhai Pass. Square City outside the Pass is so called with comparison to Crescent City, and it not only refers to the square form but also they are real city walls, which include large buildings such as Eminent Favor Hall and East or West Side-hall. In contrast, Square City of Xiao Mausoleum is only like Crescent City, which includes gable screen wall and the stairs leading to the city wall. They are different in terms of forms and functions. It can be inferred that Square City is unique to Qing mausoleums outside Shanhai Pass, and it is mausoleum architecture only Qing Dynasty possess.

羊角神兽隆恩门

方城正中南门为隆恩门，顶有三层门楼一座，俗称"五凤楼"，青砖磊筑的城墙，看起来气势威严。黄琉璃瓦顶，歇山顶的三重檐在建筑上称为"三滴水式"，据说有聚日、月、星三光，永远光明的意思。隆恩门楼面阔三间，进深七檩，建筑风格和沈阳故宫的凤凰楼颇为相似。因为努尔哈赤的属性是羊，所以隆恩门的兽面"铺首"上可以看见羊角。隆恩门券脸上雕双龙纹，腰线石上是单龙戏珠纹，下部门外为海水鱼龙，门内为云龙戏兽。门楣正中是石门额，上面镌满、蒙、汉三种文字，汉文为隆恩门。隆恩门平时不开启，只有皇帝亲临或者举行祭奠时才打开。品级不高的官员人等在门外行礼祭陵，只有亲王和贝勒才可以进门，在隆恩殿的月台上行礼。一般门洞门闩都是设在城内的，防止外人进入，隆恩门正与之相反，每当走到这，我都会想起东北人口中常说的"倒插门女婿"。倒插的隆恩门，起到了双重防护的作用。关内清陵与之相比，都没有倒插的隆恩门。永陵没有隆恩门，也没有隆恩殿，而有启运门和启运殿，这有别于福陵、昭陵。

隆恩门上的羊角神兽／左页图
Goat-horn Divine Animal on Eminent Favor Gate／Left Page
夕照隆恩门／上图
Eminent Favor Gate in Sunset／Upper

Stone Carvings of Eminent Favor Gate / Upper

Snow Scenery of Eminent Favor Gate / Right Page

EMINENT FAVOR GATE WITH A GOAT-HORN DIVINE ANIMAL

The south gate of Square City is Eminent Favor Gate (also Long'en Gate) with a three-layer gate tower, which is built upon a grey brick wall. The Gate looks stately and solemn, and the locals like to call it "Five Phoenix Tower." The gable-and-hip roof with yellow glazed tile have three eaves, which is called "three water-dripping style" in terms of architecture with such connotations as gathering lights of the sun, the moon and stars to show their eternal brightness. Eminent Favor Gate is three-room wide, seven-purlin long, and its architectural style is very similar to Phoenix House of Shenyang Imperial Palace. On Eminent Favor Gate is decorated "Pu Shou" (animal head appliqué), on which there are goat horns because Nurhaci was born in the goat year (one year in 12 year circle named after 12 animals in ancient Chinese culture). On the arch of the Gate are engraved double-dragon patterns; on the waist stone are carved patterns of single dragon playing flaming pearl; outside the lower part of Gate is fish and dragon in sea while inside the Gate is a dragon playing beasts in the cloud. In center of the lintel of Gate, inscriptions are engraved in three languages of Manchu, Mongolian and Chinese, and Chinese characters read as "隆恩门, Eminent Favor Gate." Usually, Eminent Favor Gate is not opened unless emperors come in person or when sacrifices are held. Officials who are not high enough in rank can only worship outside, and only Princes and Baylors can go through the door, worshiping on platform of Eminent Favor Gate. Door latches are usually used inside doors to prevent unwanted people from entering. Whenever I pass Eminent Favor Gate, the idea of a "married-in son-in-law" may come into my mind. Eminent Favor Gate can be latched from inside, ensuring that the building can be duly protected. In contrast, there aren't any latch located outside on Eminent Favor Gates in the mausoleums inside the Shanhai Pass. There is not Eminent Favor Gate or Eminent Favor Hall but Luck-provoking Gate and Luck-provoking Hall in Yong Mausoleum, a unique feature different from Zhaoling Imperial Tomb and Fuling Imperial Tomb.

隆恩门彩绘门匾／上图
Painted Horizontal Inscribed Board of Eminent Favor Gate / Upper

隆恩门正面九排门钉，背面无门钉／左下图、右中图
Eminent Favor Gate with Nine-row Doornails on Front-side, and no Nails on Back-side / Lower Left, Middle Right

大明楼下的装饰门钉／右下图
Doornail (for Decoration) beneath Grand Ming Tower / Lower Right

隆恩门门杠洞／右页图
Latch Hole of Eminent Favor Gate / Right Page

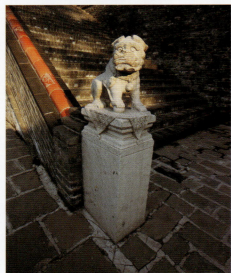

隆恩门城墙梯老照片／左上图、左下图
Old Picture of Wall Stairs of Eminent Favor Gate / Upper Left, Lower Left
隆恩门上的五凤楼楼梯／右图、右页图
Stairs of Five-phoenix Tower above Eminent Favor Gate / Right, Right Page

五凤楼内／上图
Interiors of Five-phoenix Tower / Upper

五凤楼内彩绘／右图
Colored Drawing of Five-phoenix Tower / Right

东南角楼 / 左图
Southeast Turret / Left
[长5.93米,宽5.93米,高12.5米]
(5.93 meters long, 5.93 meters wide, 12.5 meters high)

摄影的最佳视点——角楼

方城四个转角末端还建有角楼,福陵角楼采月十字脊歇山顶,正中有琉璃宝顶,全高12.54米,角楼均为两层结构,四座角楼均四面出廊,底层有拱门,楼内有木制楼梯通往二层,内外油饰彩画。站在角楼上,可俯视整座陵寝,我经常站在角楼上拍摄福陵全景。从摄影角度说,角楼是最有表现力的。特别是拍摄月牙城的时候,我腰上系着安全带,身体悬在楼角外,心想要有燕子李三的功夫就好了,拍摄就不用系安全带了。

角楼飞檐四角下各垂有铁质惊雀风铃,风吹铃动,驱赶鸟雀,使其不在这筑巢(筑巢有损建筑),方城内的建筑都用黄琉璃瓦铺顶,廊柱俱是朱红色,廊枋间有"和玺"式彩绘壁画,使整座方城显得尤为幽静、庄严、神秘而肃穆。福陵西北角楼破损比较严重,永陵没有角楼,而相比之下,昭陵角楼则保存完好。纵观清代帝王陵寝,关内清陵都没有方城,因此就没有角楼,而关内的方城都有角楼,只是这里的角楼几乎已经没有了防御功能,因为建筑比较矮,并不方便实际使用。

东南角楼／上图、右图
Southeast Turret / Upper, Right

TURRET — IDEAL SPOT OF PHOTO-TAKING

    Turrets are built at ends of the four corners of Square City. These turrets are of cross-ridge hip and gable roof, loaded with colored glazed crest in its center; they are all 12.54 meters high and of two-storyed structure; there are corridors in all four sides and arched doors on the first floor; inside the turrets, there are wooden stairs leading to the second floor with painted drawings. Standing on the turrets, one can overlook the entire mausoleum. I often stand here to shoot panoramas of Fuling Imperial Tomb. From perspective of photography, corner turrets are most expressive. In particular, when I shot Crescent City, I was then hanging outside the turrets with my waist fastened with safety belt. I am always thinking if I know Kungfu like Swallow Li San, it's unnecessary to fasten safety belt.

    There are iron-wrought bird-driving wind bells swinging under four corners of the turret cornices toscare away birds in case they nest here (nesting is detrimental to buildings). Buildings inside Square City are all roofed with yellow glazed tiles, pillars are all painted red and there are corridors are colorfully painted with frescos in forms of Seal of Harmony,

东北角楼／左图
Northeast Turret / Left
西北角楼／上图
Northwest Turret / Upper

which help present the whole Square City as particularly quiet, dignified, mysterious and solemn. The turret at the northwest is seriously damaged, and in contrast, those of Zhaoling Imperial Tomb are well protected while there isn't turret in Yong Mausoleum. Of all the mausoleums of Qing Dynasty, there are no Square Cities inside Shanhai Pass, let alone turrets. While there are turrets in Square Cities of the mausoleums outside Shanhai Pass, their defense function is almost lost, as it is not practical for use due to its relatively low buildings.

西北角楼外城墙 / 左页图
Exterior Wall of Northwest Turret / Left Page
西北角楼彩绘 / 左上图
Colored Drawing of Northwest Turret / Upper Left
西北角楼旧照 / 左下图
Old Picture of Northwest Turret / Lower Left
西北角楼 / 右图
Northwest Turret / Right

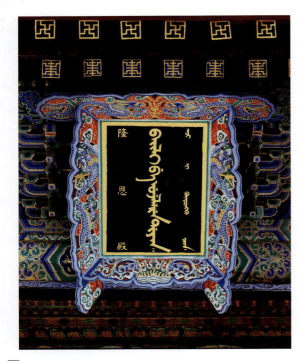

隆恩殿匾额 / 上图
Horizontal Inscribed Board of Eminent Favor Hall / Upper
隆恩殿 / 右图
Eminent Favor Hall / Right
[长22.05米，宽21.05米，高14.18米]
(22.05 meters long, 21.05 meters wide, 14.18 meters high)

为太祖帝后灵魂居住的隆恩殿

隆恩殿是清代祭祀时的主要场所，也是福陵最重要的核心建筑，取名"隆恩"，说的就是祖宗功德深厚。走进隆恩门，就可以见到坐落在须弥座式大型台基上的被称为"大殿凌云"的正殿——隆恩殿。隆恩殿，又称"享殿"，始建于康熙十六年（1677年），位居方城中，高大宽敞的汉白玉台基，须弥座、上下枋、枭及束腰，刻有花饰，台基正面"礓礤三路"（注解18），正中一路斜铺一块巨大的陛石（又名"采石"），上面雕刻"福山寿海"及"龙凤合欢"图案，寓意帝后和美，福祚绵长。相对来说，永陵的启运殿则没有栏杆也没有这些雕饰，而昭陵栏杆雕饰则更加繁华。隆恩殿为单檐歇山式建筑，面阔三间，进深二间，明间开四扇隔扇门，次次间为八槛窗，周围有十二根廊柱。殿顶铺满黄色琉璃瓦，殿脊有脊兽五个，从这也可以看出它的重要地位。隆恩殿飞檐下有蓝底金字的"隆恩殿"匾额，满文居中，蒙与汉文在左右（左右的界定，是以大行皇帝神位的角度来定的）。

隆恩殿内供奉木主神牌，殿内有大小暖阁，所谓暖阁就是由木隔扇、隔断板、天花板等在殿堂内建起的小房子，上设黄云龙缎罩顶，阁门两扇对开，

门环为赤金制成,小时候我去隆恩殿,每次看暖阁的门都是关着的,后来打开了,里面重新设宝床,陈有被、褥、枕等用品,均是帝王专用的明黄色云龙缎。大暖阁内的小暖阁,小暖阁的帘子始终没打开,不知道神龛里面究竟供奉着几个牌位,后来经允许打开一次,看见里面只供着太祖及孝慈高皇后的神牌。让我奇怪的是福陵神龛是红色的,而昭陵神龛则是绿色的。大暖阁前有龙凤宝座,宝座前面是供案,平时罩有黄云缎桌衣。供案两侧还有配案,配案后各有福金椅一把,配椅两对。供案前的五张黑漆圆形几案上是蓝色的珐琅五供一套,据说是乾隆四十三年(1778年)所制。这些都是当今的复制品,真正的文物已不知去向。而我在暖阁前的木制楼梯下,发现了一个香炉和一个烛台,均是铸铁

的，香炉上还刻有"光绪九年敬立"的字样。不知是真品还是复制品，我又放回了原处。大暖阁外侧还摆放有朝灯。值得一提的是，福陵隆恩殿反映出清陵早期建筑特点，如殿内不饰天花、梁架等木料外露，上施彩绘。天花板的使用，美观大方，增加气派。福陵隆恩殿内的柱子，中间是圆柱，两边方柱，呈"亚"字形，而昭陵隆恩殿内的柱子，而是沥粉贴金的六面体。福陵的大祭、小祭、特祭以及皇帝东巡亲自祭陵等所有祭典都在这里举行，作为祭陵中心的隆恩殿地位在福陵中自然最高。

隆恩殿／上图
Eminent Favor Hall / Upper
[台基高1.7米，周长为118米]
(with its base 1.7 meters high and perimeter 118 meters)

隆恩殿前嘲风／左一图
Chaofeng in Front of Eminent Favor Hall / Left First
景陵隆恩殿前的嘲风／左二图
Chaofeng in Front of Eminent Favor Hall in Jing Mausoleum / Left Second

EMINENT FAVOR HALL: RESTING PLACE FOR TAI TSU (EMPEROR HONG TAIJI) AND HIS EMPRESS

Eminent Favor Hall is a main sacrificial venue in Qing Dynasty and the most important core building of Fuling Imperial Tomb. The name of "Long'en" (隆恩, Eminent Favor) means great merits and virtues of ancestors. Entering Eminent Favor Gate, one can see Eminent Favor Hall on a large Sumeru-throne base, which is described as Sky Soaring Hall. Situated in Square City, Eminent Favor Hall (also referred to as Sacrificial Hall) was started to be built in the sixteenth ruling year (1677) of Emperor Kangxi. The Hall is built with lofty, spacious white marble base, on which Sumeru throne, upper and lower fangs (the first and lower layers of Sumeru), upper and lower xiao (the second layer and fourth layer) and girdle (the third layer) bear carved floral patterns. The base front has "three way Jiangca" (Note 18), the middle of which is obliquely paved with a huge sculpture stone (also called cai stone) with carved patterns of "bliss and longevity" and "joy of dragon and phoenix" implying a happy marriage and everlasting good fortune of Emperor and Empress. Comparatively speaking, there are neither rails nor such decorations in Luck-provoking Hall (also Qiyun Hall) of Yong Mausoleum while decorations in Zhaoling Imperial Tomb are more gorgeous. Eminent Favor Hall is of single-eave gable-and-hip roof, with its front aspect three bays wide and its interior two bays deep. The outer front of the Hall has installed four windows successively while two side halls respectively eight windows, along which 12 corridor pillars surround. The roof of the Hall is paved with yellow glazed tiles and there are also 5 animals sitting on the ridge, from which we can see the Hall's important position. Right under the cornice there is the horizontal board with a blue background, on which "隆恩殿" (Eminent Favor Hall) is inscribed in gold in Manchu in the middle, Mongolian on the left and Chinese on the right (which is judged from the angle of Emperor's shrine).

Wooden spirit tablets are enshrined inside Eminent Favor Hall, in which large and small cozy cabinets are divided. A cozy cabinet refers to a small room consisting of wooden partition board, partition panel and ceiling, with yellow satin of dragons and clouds covered on the top. The cabinet door is split in two and the door knocker is made of pure gold. Whenever I went there in my childhood, the doors of the cozy cabinets remained closed. Later the doors were opened, and I saw that a treasure bed inside furnished with quilt, mattress and pillows, which are all made of bright yellow satin of dragons and clouds exclusively for emperors. Inside the big cozy cabinet is a small cozy cabinet, which is never opened to the public. I didn't know how many spirit tablets were enshrined there until one time I was fortunately allowed to open the shrines and found there the spirit tablets for Emperor Tai Tsu and Empress Xiaocigao. Strangely, the shrines in Fuling Imperial Tomb are red while the ones in Zhaoling Imperial Tomb are green. In front of the large cozy cabinet, there is a throne of dragon and phoenix, before which is the altar covered by yellow cloud satin at ordinary times. On both sides of the altar are auxiliary altars, behind which there is respectively a golden chair with "fu" (福, which means blessings) and a pair of auxiliary chairs. On five round tables in black paint before the altar are a full set of five blue enamel offerings, which are said to be made in the forty-third ruling year of Emperor Qianlong (1778). However these items are just copies and the original ones are already missing. I found a censer and a candlestick under the wooden stair of the cozy cabinet, which are iron cast items with inscription of "set up in the 9th ruling year of Guangxu." I didn't know whether they were genuine items or the copies, so I put them back. In addition, royal lights are also placed outside the large cozy cabinet. It is notable that Eminent Favor Hall in Fuling Imperial Tomb reflects early architectural features of Qing mausoleums, such as undecorated ceiling, exposed wood beams with paintings. Decoration of ceilings enhances its beauty and grandness. The center pillar in the Hall is round and the ones on its two sides are square, but the ones in Zhaoling Imperial Tomb are all hexahedrons with gelled patterning and gilding. All sacrificial rites of Fuling Imperial Tomb, including big sacrifice, small sacrifice, special sacrifice and Emperor's sacrifice on their eastward worship tour, are held here. Therefore, as center of sacrifices, Hall of Eminent Favor naturally enjoys highest status in Fuling Imperial Tomb.

隆恩殿／左图
Eminent Favor Hall / Left
隆恩殿旧貌／上图
Former State of Eminent Favor Hall / Upper

努尔哈赤的圣德神功

努尔哈赤，为什么受到世界史学界的重视，就是因为他是女真族，女真族在中国现今五十六个民族中早已不存在。

努尔哈赤，是女真族建州部子孙，爱新觉罗氏，明嘉靖三十八年（1559年）出生于辽东苏子河流域的建州左卫，从小受继母虐待。努尔哈赤，满语是野猪皮的意思。努尔哈赤的父亲"塔克世"是明朝建州左卫指挥使，10岁时，母亲喜塔喇氏病故后，十几岁便与父亲分家。后来，他投身明朝总兵李成梁帐下，作战勇猛、屡立战功。

其实努尔哈赤也是个孝子，他的父亲对他不好，童年过得可谓辛酸，他还能够为父报仇，修建陵寝，成就大业者，一般都有仁孝的一面，孝感动天，而我在序言里就说过努尔哈赤的仁。关于努尔哈赤的仁，有史料可查的很多。比如有记载，在万历十二年九月时，努尔哈赤率兵攻打翁科洛城，被守城勇士鄂尔果尼射伤，还有一个叫科罗的守城士兵，潜到努尔哈赤近处，射伤他的脖颈，攻城只好撤退。攻城后将二人生擒，众将欲将之处死，努尔哈赤却说："两敌交锋，志在取胜。彼为其主射我；今为我用，不又为我射敌乎。"说罢，亲为二人解绑，收为部下。还有一个故事，就是曾有刺客潜入努尔哈赤住所行刺。努尔哈赤将其拿下。侍卫要斩刺客，努尔哈赤却大声喝问："尔非盗牛来耶？"刺客顺势回答是来盗牛，努尔哈赤就把他放走了。可见努尔哈赤的大度宽仁不是常人能比的。而他的孝，在谥号里也

有体现。值得一提的是，清朝历代皇帝的谥号中都含有一个孝字，清朝以武得天下，以孝治天下，因此，在陵寝规制上，一般都比前朝递减，以示孝道。

明万历四十四年（1616年），努尔哈赤在新宾赫图阿拉城建立大金国，年号"天命"。天命三年（1618年），努尔哈赤以"七大恨"（注解20）为由起兵反明。在著名的"萨尔浒大战"后，努尔哈赤逆转了明强金弱的局势，先后占领开原、铁岭、沈阳、辽阳、北宁等地，至万历四十七年(1619年)，努尔哈赤平灭叶赫，基本上统一女真诸部。明朝在今东北地区设立三个卫所，分别称作建州，海西和野人，分设督司受明总兵节制，因此以地域划分为三部女真，称野人女真、建州女真和海西女真。实际上他们彼此之间不一定有血统关系。海西女真的叶赫部源自蒙古边缘部落。野人女真与金朝的女真族有较近的血统关系，努尔哈赤所在的满洲是建州女真其中一个部族的名称。满洲崛起，征服了东北各部族，才统一称谓为"满洲"，其中包括了归顺满洲的蒙古人、朝鲜人及辽东汉人。努尔哈赤经过三十六年征抚，结束了女真内部四百年来彼此征杀的局面。在统一女真诸部的过程中，努尔哈赤在女真人原有狩猎组织牛录的基础上，创建了八旗制度，以旗统军、以旗统民，将女真社会的军事、政治、经济、行政、司法等融为一体，为入关和开国奠定了坚实的基础，也为一个新民族登上历史舞台做好了一切准备。

然而，"攻无不克战无不胜"的努尔哈赤，在天命十一年（1626年）3月率军攻打宁远时，遇到年轻将领袁崇焕，打了他一生中唯一的一次败仗。努尔哈赤遣被俘汉人入城，谕告袁崇焕："吾以二十万众攻此城，破之必矣，尔众官若降，即封以高爵。"遭到袁的严词拒绝。正月二十四日，努尔哈赤下令，全军猛烈进攻。袁崇焕率领兵民拼死反抗，"枪炮药罐雷石齐下"，努尔哈赤连攻两天，未能克城，伤亡惨重，"攻具焚弃，丧失殆尽"，著名的宁远之战，以明军的胜利金兵的失败而结束。同年8月11日，努尔哈赤死于现今于洪区翟家乡大埃金堡浑河水域，终年68岁。关于努尔哈赤的逝去，众说纷纭，有人说因为炮伤，也有人说是因为他背后恶疮发作。我个人认为，他不可能因为炮伤去世，明朝正史中也没有任何记载，却有资料记载天命十一年四月，努尔哈赤亲率大军征蒙古。如果重伤,怎么可能还带兵打仗？天命十一年8月12日，努尔哈赤葬于沈阳城内西北角；天聪三年，正式安葬于福陵。

努尔哈赤一生，25岁起兵，68岁故去，戎马生涯44年，战功卓著自不用说。而西方人最关注中国历史上的两位英雄，一个是成吉思汗，另一个就是努尔哈赤。因为他这样一个生活在边塞没有上过私塾的人，后来能够建立后金，并播下"康乾盛世"的种子。这种成就与命运都是非同寻常的。另外，作为中国众多兄弟民族中的女真族首领，率领满洲民族人口三百余万（女真人仅二十万），能够渐渐强大，统领整个中国近1亿5千万人口，而当时汉族人口已达八千余万，这也是一件不可思议的事情。汉族一直是中国民族的主体，在五千年的历史发展中，无疑起着主导作用。但是，中国历史上的兄弟民族称帝者也不在少数，南北朝北魏孝文帝元宏是鲜卑族人，辽太祖耶律阿保机是契丹人，西夏景宗李元昊是党项族人，元世祖忽必烈，成吉思汗的孙子，是蒙古人族人。尽管连孔子都有："夷狄之有君，不如诸夏之亡也。"对兄弟民族的蔑视可谓溢于言表，然而也正是孔子所说的这些"夷狄"建立了疆域广阔的大清王朝。从整个历史进程来看，兄弟民族和汉族一样，同样都在推进历史的发展和人类文明的进步中，贡献了自己的一份力量。人口的多少决定不了地位的高低，民族之间本不该有高低贵贱之分。

女真族，在宋辽西夏金的时候，成立了金国政权（1115-1234年），存在119年，而410年后，女真族后代努尔哈赤又复建立了金国政权，历史上称为后金。努尔哈赤的儿子皇太极统一长城以北，融合北方民族成立了满族，孙子顺治进北京入主中原，曾孙康熙平定三藩，收复台湾，统一中国。如果没有努尔哈赤奠定基础，清王朝是不可能成为中华民族的伟大继承者的。

隆恩殿内／左页图
Interiors of Eminent Favor Hall／Left Page
[外檐彩画为最高等级的和玺彩画，殿内彩画不设天花，而是在裸露的梁檩上直接绘画，与沈阳故宫的崇政殿彩画做法相同。这种做法谓"彻上明造"是关外早期建筑特点之一]
(Its outer eaves are colorfully painted with Seals of Harmony as the state of art permits at that time. The inner Hall is not decorated with ceilings for interior color painting, which instead are executed directly on the exposed beams and purlins, the same method of color painting as adopted for Chongzheng Hall of Shenyang. This method is called "Exposed Ceiling Construction," one of the architectural features outside Shanhai Pass at its early stage)

太祖武皇帝朝服像（努尔哈赤）、孝慈高皇后像（叶赫那拉孟古）／下图
Drawings of Emperor Nurhaci in Court Dress and Empress Xiaocigao (Yehe Nara Menggu)／Lower

VIRTUES AND DEEDS OF GREAT NURHACI

The reason why Nurhaci is valued by historians in the world is simply that he is a Jurchen, which does not exist anymore among the fifty-six nationalities of China.

Nurhaci, descendent of Jurchen in Jianzhou, surnamed Aisin Gioro, was born in the thirty-eighth ruling year (1559) of Emperor Jiajing of Ming Dynasty in Zuowei of Jianzhou along Suzi River in Liaodong Peninsula. Nurhaci means skin of wild pig in Manchu. Takeshi, father of Nurhaci, was commander of Zuowei of Jianzhou in Ming Dynasty. When he was ten years old, Nurhaci's mother died from an illness. After that, he was always abused by his stepmother. Later, he was committed to serving Li Chengliang, commander-in-chief of Ming Dynasty and fought bravely to make himself distinguished in battlefields.

In fact, Nurhaci is a filial son to his father, and he tried to revenge and built a mausoleum for his father, although he was ill-treated in his bitter childhood. Generally speaking, a winner, especially one who has accomplished great cause, tends to show a side of benevolence and filial piety, which I've already mentioned in the preface. As to Nurhaci, there are a lot of such historical data worth study. For example, it is recorded that in September of the 12th ruling year of Emperor Wanli, Nurhaci was shot by a warrior Erguoni in attacking Wengkeluo City, and another defending soldier named Keluo shot his neck at a very close distance, which led to their retreat. These two soldiers were captured alive later after the siege, and his subordinates advocated executing them, but Nurhaci said, "two forces fight for the aim to win. He shot me for his Lord; if he is my subordinate, I dare to say he will shoot enemies for me". Then, he untied them in person and accepted them as his subordinates. There is another story that there was an assassin who sneaked into Nurhachi's residence to kill him. Nurhaci captured him. The guards were about to chop the assassin, but Nurhaci asked loudly, "Aren't you here to steal cattle?" So the assassin replied that he did want to steal cattle, and Nurhaci let him go. We could conclude how generous and benevolent Nurhaci is. And his piety is thoroughly shown in the posthumous title. It is worth mentioning that all the posthumous titles of Qing emperors have a word piety. Qing Dynasty gained its sovereignty by force and its emperors reigned the country with piety. So the scales of later mausoleums decrease in order to show filial piety towards former emperors.

In the forty-fourth ruling year (1616) of Emperor Wanli of Ming Dynasty, Nurhaci founded Great Jin Kingdom in Hetuala (today's Xinbin of Liaoning Province) with the reign title of "Tianming." In the third year of Tianming (1618), Nurhaci rose in arms against Ming Dynasty on account of "Seven Hatreds" (Note 20). Following Battle of Saerhu, Nurhaci reversed the situation that Jin was weaker than Ming, and occupied such places as Kaiyuan, Tieling, Shenyang, Liaoyang and Beining in succession. Up to the forty-seventh ruling year of Emperor Wanli (1619), Nurhaci eliminated Yehe and almost unified all Jurchen tribes. Ming Dynasty set up three garrisons under control of commander-in-chief in today's northeast region, Jianzhou, Haixi and Yeren (Barbarian), according to which Jurchen tribes were divided into three tribes: Jianzhou Jurchen, Haixi Jurchen and Barbarian Jurchen. However, there wasn't any kinship among these three tribes. It is studied that Yehe tribe of Haixi Jurchen came from Mongolia and there was close kinship between Yeren Jurchen and Jurchen of Jin State. Manchu where Nurhaci belong was actually a tribe of Jianzhou Jurchen. After conquering all tribes in northeast China, they began to call themselves "Manchu" as a whole, including some Mongolians, Koreans and Han nationalities there. After thirty-six years of conquering, he ended the situation that Jurchen tribes fought internally over three hundred years. During the unification of Jurchen tribes, Nurhaci had established System of Eight Banners based on their original hunting organization of Jurchen people - Niru. Under such system, armed forces and masses were unified while military, politics, economics, administration and judiciary were integrated, which laid a solid foundation for advancing to south of Shanhai Pass and establishing a new state and prepared everything for a new nationality to appear on historical stage.

However, when ever-victorious Nurhaci led his forces to attack Ningyuan in March of the eleventh ruling year of Tianming (1626), he encountered Yuan Chonghuan, a young general and suffered the only defeat in his life. Nurhaci sent Han captives to tell Yuan Chonghuan: "If I attack your city with forces of two hundred thousand soldiers, it will definitely be breached; if you officials surrender, you will be awarded high noble ranks." Mr. Yuan refused it with harsh words. On 24 of Lunar January, Nurhaci ordered all his forces to attack fiercely. Yuan Chonghuan led his soldiers and masses to resist desperately by using guns, stones and everything in hands. For consecutive two days, Nurhaci attacked in vain and suffered serious casualties; in addition, all weapons were burned and totally lost. The well-known Ningyuan Battle ended in triumph of Ming forces. On August 11 of the same year, Nurhaci died at the age of 68 in Hun River Basin of Daaijinbao Village of Zhaijiaxiang Town in Yuhong Region. Opinions are widely different about death of Nurhaci. Some people hold that it was due to gun wounds while others hold that it was caused by back ulcer. In my personal view, it is impossible that he died from gun wounds and no relevant records can be found in biographical history books of Ming Dynasty. On the contrary, some data recorded that in April of the eleventh ruling year of Tianming, Nurhaci led forces to fight in Mongolia.

If he had suffered a serious wound, how would he have led forces at war? Nurhaci was buried in the northwest corner of Shenyang on August 12 of the eleventh year of Tianming and was officially buried in Fuling Imperial Tomb in the third ruling year of Emperor Tiancong.

Uprising at 25 and died at 68, Nurhaci had a military life of 44 years and made numerous contributions, which were summarized by some scholars as ten major ones. Westerners are most concerned with two heroes in Chinese history: Genghis Khan and Nurhaci. Though living in the frontier area and receiving no private school education, he could establish Later Jin and sow seeds for the heyday of Qing Dynasty from reigns of Kangxi to Qianlong. This achievement and fate are quite extraordinary and incredible. In addition, as a Jurchen ethnic leader in China, he led Manchu ethnic population of over three hundred million, including only two hundred thousand Jurchen people, to becoming a strong nation and then reigned the entire Chinese population of nearly 150 million, among which Han population reached eighty million. Although Han nationality undoubtedly plays a leading role in the five thousand years of historical development as the main body of Chinese nation, emperors of ethnic minorities are not few. Emperor Xiaowen (Yuanhong) of North Wei is of Xianbei nationality; Yelv ABaoJi, Founder of Liao Dynasty, is a Khitan; Emperor Jing Zong (Li Yuanhao) of West Xia is from Dangxiang ethnic minority; Kublai Khan, grandson of Genghis Khan, is a Mongolian. Even though Confucius once said, "barbarians even with rulers are not as good as Xia Dynasty without a ruler," which expresses his contempt to minorities, those "barbarians" Confucius mentioned established Qing Dynasty with vast territory. Viewing from the entire historical process, ethnic minorities, like Han nationality, contribute their efforts in promoting development of history and progress of human civilization. The number of population can not decide status of an ethnic group, and there should not be any distinction of the noble and the humble among different nationalities.

Jurchen established the regime of Jin Nation (1115 — 1234), which existed for 119 years along with Song, Liao and West Xia and Jin. 410 years later, Nurhaci, descendant of Jurchen, reestablished Jin Nation, historically known as Later Jin. Hong Taiji, son of Nurhaci unified the north of Great Wall, integrated all the races into a new established Manchu; Shunzhi, his grandson entered Beijing to reign Central Plains; Kangxi, his great grandson, put the Three Seigneurs down and recovered Taiwan to re-unify China. If there wasn't such solid foundation established by Nurhaci, Qing Dynasty couldn't become a great successor to Chinese civilization.

太祖武皇帝（努尔哈赤）神位、孝慈高皇后（叶赫那拉孟古）神位／下图
Memorial Tablets of Emperor Nurhaci and Empress Xiaocigao (Yehe Nara Menggu) / Lower

建州与叶赫的爱恨情仇

努尔哈赤一生娶了十六位妃子，他十八岁时就与佟佳氏哈哈纳札青成婚。建州与叶赫世代都有亲缘关系，据说努尔哈赤的外祖也是叶赫人。在努尔哈赤二十九岁时，娶了叶赫的孟古哲哲，孟古实际上是他的第四位妻子。就是这个叶赫纳拉氏与爱新觉罗氏，说不清理还乱的爱恨情仇。

孟古，叶赫纳拉氏，孟古生于明朝万历三年（1575年），父亲杨吉努，为海西叶赫部首领。明万历三十一年（1603年），杨吉努见努尔哈赤英姿勃勃、相貌非常，便将女儿孟古许诺努尔哈赤"堪为君配"，孟古14岁时由哥哥亲自送往与努尔哈赤"缔姻"。明万历二十年（1592年）10月25日，孟古生一子，取名"皇太极"，三十五年后继承汗位，四十五年后他成了中国历史上又一位皇帝。明万历三十一年，孟古病故，终年29岁，一生只有皇太极一子，是努尔哈赤第八个儿子。当时建州与叶赫关系紧张，孟古病危前有个心愿，就是想见母亲一面，努尔哈赤派人前往叶赫，孟古的哥哥纳林布禄拒绝了接走他母亲的请求，努尔哈赤大怒。从此，努尔哈赤与叶赫的关系破裂。孟古死后，努尔哈赤为她举行了盛大祭礼并将她葬在自家院内3年，第4年才迁葬于尼亚满山冈，在那儿为她建陵，派觉尔察氏一户看守。努尔哈赤死后，皇太极继承"汗位"，孟古因此成为"皇太后"。天聪三年，皇太极在沈阳城东石咀头山营造福陵，将太祖努尔哈赤与孟古"合葬"。努尔哈赤有十六个儿子，怎么会让叶赫的外孙继承汗位，这成为历史难解之谜。

提起努尔哈赤的婚姻，就不能不提到另外一个叶赫那拉氏的女人，东哥。东哥又被叫做叶赫老女，也是叶赫第一美女，与她有关的种种传说中，最著名的就要属"一女灭四国"（注解21）了。东哥的父亲是布斋，布斋死于努尔哈赤与九部联军之战，尸体被砍为两半，一半交还叶赫，一半带回建州。所以东哥是孟古的堂侄女，努尔哈赤对她而言算是杀父仇人。东哥声言："努尔哈赤是杀父仇人，誓死不嫁，谁若杀死努尔哈赤，便嫁谁为妻"。于是，布扬古贝勒当众毁约，并向海西各部征婚，条件是杀死努尔哈赤。结果那些向东哥求婚的部落，都被努尔哈赤所灭。当年我曾专门到过叶赫部的遗址吉林四平市叶赫镇考察过。万历四十七年（1619年）平灭叶赫，叶赫酋长金台吉临死前发下的诅咒："即使我叶赫族里只剩下一个女人，也要将建州女真灭亡！"

叶赫那拉部的女人，总是跟爱新觉罗家族的关键时刻联系在一起。除了孟古、东哥，叶赫那拉氏还在清王朝即将覆灭的时候为其提供了慈禧和隆裕两位皇后，而清帝国在慈禧的主政下迈向衰亡，最终签署清帝退位条约的就是慈禧太后的侄女——隆裕皇太后。同时，似乎应验了叶赫部传说的诅咒："兴也叶赫，亡也叶赫"。这两个家族的关系，真可谓错综复杂而又变幻莫测。只是中国历朝都有意把亡国的责任推到女人身上，像商纣王的宠妃妲己、周幽王的褒姒、吴国的西施、汉成帝的赵飞燕、唐明皇的杨玉环，都是男人的替罪羊。女人有什么错呢？错的是那些不知进取的君王才对。清朝的灭亡与叶赫也没有决定性联系，叶赫文化是中华民族文化的重要组成部分，它对研究东北民族史与边疆史有重要意义，是我们应该深入研究的重要课题。

（原文《我的叶赫五项观点》发表于中国吉林叶赫国际研讨会）

雪漫福陵三大殿／左页图
Three Temples of Fuling Imperial Tomb in Boundless Snow / Left Page
清东陵（定东陵）隆恩殿／下图
Eminent Favor Hall of East Qing Mausoleum (East Ding Mausoleum) / Lower

LOVE AND HATE BETWEEN JIANZHOU AND YEHE

In his lifetime, Nurhaci married sixteen concubines in total. At age of 18, he married Dongjia Hahanazhaqing. There were marriage relations for generations between Jianzhou and Yehe. It is said the father of Nurhaci's mother was also from Yehe. At age of 29, Nurhaci married Menggu Sister of Yehe, who is actually the fourth wife of Nurhaci. It is this Yehenala that had a complex relation with Aisin Gioro.

Menggu surnamed Yehe Nala was born in the third ruling year of Emperor Wanli of Ming Dynasty (1575) and her father, Yang Jinu, was head of Yehe tribe in Haixi. In the thirty-first ruling year of Emperor Wanli (1603), seeing that Nurhaci looked handsome and unusual, Yang Jinu promised to marry her daughter Menggu Sister to him. When Menggu was fourteen years old, her elder brother sent her in person to Nurhaci for marriage. On October 25 of the twentieth year ruling of Emperor Wanli (1592), Menggu Sister gave birth to the eighth prince, named Hong Taiji, who became emperor 45 years later. In the thirty-first ruling year of Emperor Wanli, Menggu Sister died from an illness at age of 29 when Jianzhou had an intense relationship with Yehe. Menggu had a wish before she was critically ill, namely to see her mother.

Nurhaci sent for her mother in Yehe, but got refused by Menggu's elder brother Nalinbulu. Nurhaci was furious. After death of Menggu, Nurhaci held a grand sacrificial ceremony for her and buried her in his own yard. She remained there for three years until in the fourth year tho tomb was moved to Niyaman Hillock, where a mausoleum was built and a family surnamed Jueercha were assigned to keep watch. After Nurhaci died, Hong Taiji succeeded him as Khan and Menggu Sister became Empress Dowager. In the third year of Tiancong, Hong Taiji built Fuling Imperial Tomb in Mount Shizuitou, east of Shenyang and buried Tai Tsu and Menggu Sister together. Nurhaci had 16 sons, however, why did he let grandson of Yehe to inherit the Crown. It is an enigma of history.

Speaking of Nurhaci's marriage, another woman surnamed Yehe Nala, Dongge has to be mentioned. Dongge, also called Youngest Daughter of Yehe, was No.1 beauty of her tribe. Of her various stories, the best known was the "one woman ruined four kingdoms" (Note 21). Dongge's father Buzhai died in the battle between Nurhaci and the alliance of nine tribes. His body was cut in two halves, with one half returned to Yehe and the other taken back to Jianzhou. Though Dongge was niece of Menggu, Nurhaci was her enemy who had killed her father. Dongge claimed, "Nurhaci is my enemy who killed my father,

隆恩殿东侧四扇窗、东西两扇门（局部）／左页图
Four Windows of East Eminent Favor Hall, and its East and West Doors (Partial) / Left Page

福陵隆恩殿丹碧石／右上图
Red and Green Jade inside Eminent Favor Hall of Fuling Imperial Tomb / Upper Right

福陵隆恩殿拜石／右下图
Worship Stone inside Eminent Favor Hall of Fuling Imperial Tomb / Lower Right

and I promise to marry nobody until someone kills him; I will marry whoever kills Nurhaci." As a result, Dongge's brother, Buyanggu Baylor, broke engagement before the public and sought marriage among various Haixi tribes on condition that the would-be husband would kill Nurhaci. However, those tribes proposing to Dongge were all wiped out by Nurhaci. I inspected specifically at the site of the ancient ruins of Yehe tribe in Yehe town od Siping city in Jilin province. In the 47th ruling year of Emperor Wanli (1619), Yehe tribe was seized, and its chief Jintaiji made a curse before dying, "even if there is only one woman left in our tribe, she will ruin Jianzhou Jurchen!"

Women in Yehe Nala tribe were always related with Aisin Gioro clan at critical moments. These two clans had complex and changeable relations. In addition to Menggu and Dongge, two Empresses of Cixi and Longyu on eve of the collapse of Qing Dynasty were from the same tirbe, which complies with the saying "rise up due to Yehe and fall due to Yehe," because it was under Cixi's control that Qing Dynasty came to collapse and it was her niece Longyu who subscribed Treaty of Abdication for Emperor. People throughout Chinese dynasties just intentionally blame women for ruin of a dynasty, such as King Zhou's concubine Daji in Shang Dynasty, King You's Baosi in Zhou Dynasty, Xishi in Kingdom Wu, Emperor Chengsi's Zhao Feiyan in Han Dynasty and Yang Yuhuan in Tang Dynasty, who are all the scapegoats of men. What wrong did these women do? The lazy and dissolute emperors are those who did the wrong things. The ruin of Qing Dynasty has nothing to do with Yehe tribe. Yehe culture is also an important part of Chinese culture, which attaches great importance to researching Northeast ethnical history and frontier history. It is an important subject we should study thoroughly.

(The original version of My Five Points of View on Yehe Tribe is published in International Symposium on Yehe Tribe held in Jilin, China)

为何用亲生子女联姻

努尔哈赤一生与外戚的关系都不和，而他的儿子皇太极则正相反。虽然都是政治联姻，但是，努尔哈赤对外戚都是征伐，皇太极却与外戚们的关系很好。可能，这不仅是由于父子两人性格不同的缘故，也是由政治局势需要所致。不过，提到政治联姻，不能不说，中国历史上那些著名的通婚，如文成公主入藏，昭君出塞，并不是皇帝的亲生女儿，只不过是并无血缘关系的义女，所以，很多时候，通婚的效果并不如皇帝预想的那样成功，边疆战事仍然接连不断，始终为朝廷隐患。而努尔哈赤不仅自己娶蒙古女人，也鼓励自己的子孙后代娶蒙古女人，也将自己的亲生女儿嫁去蒙古，这样，形成了实实在在的亲戚关系。"打断骨头连着筋"，再互相征伐也不至于灭族。和中国古代的相同，英国女王伊丽莎白就是通过皇室与整个欧洲的联姻，使欧洲大陆都有了她的血统，成为整个欧洲的外祖母。用亲生子女联姻，这在历史上也是一种进步。所以当时在清朝甚至有"满蒙是一家"的说法。其实，清以后，各民族之间风俗习惯的相互影响，特别是上层贵族的民族通婚，形成一种导向，以上行下效的潮流推动了民间的民族通婚，形成了民族大融合。

清朝的通婚，虽然有严格的规定，在八旗中有一种叫"旗民不结亲"的风俗，在满族内部又被称为"满汉不通婚"。严格来讲"满汉不通婚"并不是指满族人不能与汉族人结婚，而是指八旗内部可以通婚，但是旗人不可以与旗外人结亲。比如顺治与佟妃，佟妃的祖辈与父辈都是汉人，但因都是清朝的开国功臣，后成为汉族旗人，所以他们可以通婚，而他们的儿子就是大名鼎鼎的康熙皇帝。而乾隆帝也曾把自己的女儿嫁给孔子后人，至今在孔林内还有于氏坊。对于有严格律法限制的满汉婚姻都有例外，何况于周边民族之间呢。

有时候，我们不能孤立地去看一个民族，也不能严格地界定一个民族，兄弟民族是一家，都是同胞，又何必分得那么清楚，非得分出个你我、大小、多少呢。从现在的角度看建州与叶赫之争好比历史上的炎黄之战，可以说是兄弟之争，蚩尤则是部落之争，汉匈是融和之争。所有的战争，最后都是为了推进中国历史的进步而产生的，是战争也是变革。我认为清朝的历代帝王，不仅认为自己是国家，连自己的子女都是国家的，为了国家利益都要听从国家的安排，已经没有个人利益了，用亲生子女联姻这一点，就可以证明。

隆恩殿前狮子／左页图
Stone Lion in Front of Eminent Favor Hall / Left Page

IMMEDIATE RELATIVES FOR INTER-MARRIAGE

Nurhaci were on bad terms with his in-laws during his life, as opposite to the case with his son Hong Taiji. Although both married for political purposes, Nurhaci went to attack such relatives while Hong Taiji had good relations with them, which possibly resulted from different personalities of between father and son and demands of the political situation. However, referring to political marriages, we have to think of such well-known political marriages in Chinese history as Princess Wencheng into Tibet and Zhaojun exiting the fortress, but they were not birth daughters of the emperors, but adopted ones without any blood relationship. Therefore, effect of such marriages was not as successful as expected most of the time; the border wars still continues, and they are always the hidden trouble of royal court. However, Nurhaci not only married Mongolian women himself, but also encouraged his own sons and grandsons to marry Mongolian women, and he also sent his daughters to Mongolia; consequently, the real relationship of relatives was formed. The conquest will not go to genocide, because "although bones are broken their tendons are with attached." Similar to the ancient China, Queen Elizabeth of United Kingdom has her lineage all over the European continent through the intermarriage of royal families in Europe, and she becomes grandmother of Europe. Intermarriages with biological children are also a kind of progress in history. Therefore, there is even a saying in Qing Dynasty that "Manchu and Mongolian are one united family." In fact, influenced by the customs between various ethnics, especially by the upper nobility intermarriages, an orientation is formed to promote trend of nationality intermarriages and ethnical fusion.

There are strict rules of intermarriage among Eight Banners in Qing Dynasty that "no marriage between banners and civilians," which is also called "no intermarriage between Manchu and Han nationality" inside Manchu. Strictly speaking, it does not mean that Manchu and Han people can not marry one another, but that they can only within Eight Banners, and marriage between inside the Banners and outside the Banners is not allowed. Let's take an example of Emperor Shunzhi and Imperial Concubine Tong, whose grandparents and parents were all in Han nationality. Yet since Tong's grandparents and parents were founding courtiers of Qing Dynasty and they became banners with Han nationality, Emperor Shunzhi was allowed to marry Tong, and their son was famous Emperor Kangxi. Emperor Qianlong let her daughter marry descendant of Confucius, and now Yushi Fang is still in Confucian Garden. There are still exceptions within those strictly limited Manchu and Han marriages, not to mention among neighboring ethnics.

Sometimes, we can not simply treat an ethnic in isolation, or strictly define an ethnic; all the brother ethnics are fellow citizens, why should we tell them from each other? From the current perspective, wars between Jianzhou and Yehe can be defined as struggles between brothers just like wars between Emperor Yan and Emperor Huang, while wars between Emperor Huang and Emperor Chiyou is tribal dispute, and Han and Hun fought for fusion. In long run, all wars are born for promoting progress of Chinese history, a kind of reform. I think that Qing emperors think that not only they themselves, but also their own children belong to their nation. For the sake of benefit of the whole country, they all have to obey national needs, leaving no personal interests, which can be proved from intermarriage with their own children.

帝后灵魂暂居的东配殿

在隆恩殿的两侧，以神道为轴左右对称排列着两座建筑，仿佛是隆恩殿的左膀右臂，极好地衬托出隆恩殿的重要地位，这就是福陵的东配殿和西配殿。东配殿在隆恩殿东厢，在陵寝中的地位仅次于隆恩殿。东配殿为歇山式建筑，顶铺黄色琉璃瓦，殿脊有3个脊兽，四面出廊，其下有低矮的石基座，比起昭陵，福陵东西配殿距离城墙很近，殿角几乎搭在城墙上，离墙仅1.25米。门窗梁柱朱漆彩绘，殿内原有小暖间及宝座等一些陈设。东配殿用来存放祝版和制帛。隆恩殿大修时，也存放神牌。东配殿作为配殿，但在特殊的情况下却可以代替隆恩殿。当隆恩殿进行大修时，为防止惊扰太祖和孝慈高皇后的在天之灵，要将殿内供奉的太祖、孝慈高皇后两座神牌由隆恩殿迁至东配殿暂时供奉，等待隆恩殿竣工之后重新将神牌请回。我原来以为东西配殿是存放妃子牌位的，后来研究知道，除了皇后，妃子们是根本没有资格进到红墙内的。福陵有一个寿康妃园寝，在福陵西北的后陵前堡村。康寿妃是努尔哈赤的一个侧福晋，一生无子嗣，因为活得年龄较大，历经了天命、天聪、崇德、顺治、康熙五朝，这在清代妃子中绝无仅有的一个妃子。而昭陵有一个贵妃园，宸妃、懿靖大贵妃园寝，因为多次被盗和历史缘故，毁坏比较严重，几乎找不到当年的遗址，2003年我还曾经参与过挖掘。

而隆恩殿恭请神牌是福陵一种大礼，皇帝要钦派宗室或盛京将军主持，其他人无资格随便请神牌。直到完工以后，还要举行仪式将神牌重新请回隆恩殿。同时，在神牌供奉于东配殿期间，所有应按例进行的大小祭祀，一律按制在东配殿举行，不可偏废。如，乾隆三十年（1770年）五月隆恩殿大修，高宗钦命宗室永玮、都统四格会同盛京将军舍图肯将神牌移到东配殿。高宗要求永玮在盛京等候，工程完竣将神牌重新请回隆恩殿方允永玮回京交差。所以，东配殿的作用是福陵内任何一座建筑都无法取代的。

东配殿的另一项重要功用就是存放祝帛与祝版。所谓祝帛，就是一种用丝绸制成的帛条，上面书写着皇帝的祭词。而祝版则是祭祀时专门放置祝文的用具，其形制是一块约一尺见方的长方形木板，白底儿，四周镶有黄绫边，中间贴祝文。这两件祭祀用品都是表达皇帝哀思以示孝道的文书，地位崇高。祭陵的前一天需由盛京礼部送至福陵备用，其存放的地点就是东配殿。第二天举行祭祀前，祝帛要请至隆恩殿内，放在供案上专门用来盛帛的筐内（注解19）；祝版则要读祝官等至东配殿供祝版的几案前，行一跪三叩头礼后，捧祝版出殿，由正中神道来到隆恩殿西廊下的供案前跪下，将所捧之祝版供于案上，再行一跪三叩头礼后，礼部官员才能恭请神牌，开始祭奠。

EAST SIDE-HALL WHERE SPIRIT OF EMPRESS RESIDES

On both sides of Eminent Favor Hall, two buildings are arranged in bilateral symmetry with Spirit Path as the axis, which are East Side-hall and West Side-hall. Just like right and left hands they wonderfully highlight the status of Eminent Favor Hall. East Side-hall is in the east wing of Eminent Favor Hall, just inferior to Eminent Favor Hall in the Mausoleum. It is a building of hip-and-gable roof with yellow glazed tiles on its top, on which ridge there are three ridge animals. And it is built on low stone base with porches on its four sides. Compared with Zhaoling Imperial Tomb, the two side halls are very close to city wall, which is only 1.25 meters away. Pictures are painted on its doors, windows, beams and columns in red lacquer, and small cozy cabinets and thrones used to furnished inside. East Side-hall was used to house prayer boards and prayer silks, and also spirit tablets when Eminent Favor Hall was being overhauled. Though it was a side hall at normal times, East Side-hall could replace Eminent Favor Hall on special occasions. When Eminent Favor Hall was overhauled, the two spirit tablets for Emperor Tai Tsu and Empress Xiaocigao would be moved here for temporary enshrinement and later be ceremonially returned after its completion of overhauling. I had thought the side halls were used for

memorial tablets of concubines. But I learn from the later study that concubines are not allowed to be put here in the red wall except for empresses. There is a Concubine Garden in Qianbao Village, northwest of Fuling Imperial Tomb. Concubine Kangshou, a side Fujin of Nurhachi, lived the five reigns of Tianming, Tiancong, Chongde, Shunzhi and Kangxi. She was the only concubine who enjoyed this honor in Qing Dynasty. There is also a Noble Concubines Garden in Zhaoling Imperial Tomb, where Concubine Chen, Imperial Consort Yijing are buried here. But its site could hardly be found due to damages of grave-robberies and historical incidents. I was once fortunate to participate in its unearthing.

As inviting spirit tablets was a solemn ceremony in Fuling Imperial Tomb, Emperor would assign a member of the imperial clan or general in Shengjing to chair the ceremony, and without authorization, others were disqualified in this regard. After completion of overhauling, a ceremony would be held to return spirit tablets to Eminent Favor Hall. In addition, while spirit tablets were temporarily enshrined in East Side-hall, all sacrifices, whether small and large, must be performed in East Side-hall according to rules and couldn't be neglected. For instance, Eminent Favor Hall was overhauled in May of the thirtieth ruling year of Emperor Qianlong (1770), Emperor ordered Yong Wei (a member of the imperial clan), Si Ge (Dutong, a military commander) and She Tuken (Shengjing general) to move spirit tablets to East Side-hall. Emperor asked Yong Wei to wait in Shengjing until completion of overhauling to return spirit tablets to Eminent Favor Hall before returning to Beijing to report on his mission. Therefore, the role of East Side-hall was irreplaceable by any other buildings in Fuling Imperial Tomb.

Another important function of East Side-hall is to store prayer silks and prayer boards. A prayer silk refers to the silk strip with Emperor's written funeral oration on it. A prayer board is a special tool for the elegiac address to stick to at the time of sacrifice. It is a rectangle wooden board of about one square Chinese foot with a white background, and the board is bordered with yellow damask silk and the elegiac address is stuck in its middle. These two sacrificial items are both texts expressing Emperor's grief to show his filial piety, thus enjoying a lofty status. On the day before sacrificing to the Mausoleum, Shengjing Board of Rites and Ceremonies needs to send them to Fuling Imperial Tomb for preparation, and the storing place is East Side-hall. Next day these prayer silks must be invited to Hall of Eminent Favor and be put into a "fei" (篚 , which is a kind of basket, Note 19) on the altar; as for sprayer boards, prayer readers must perform the rite of one kneeling and three kowtows before prayer boards on the long enshrinement table in East Side-hall and then went out of the Hall with them in both hands. Then they walked through Spirit Path in the middle to kneel down before the altar under the west corridor of Eminent Favor Hall, put sprayer boards on the altar, and performed the rite of one kneeling and three kowtows. After that, officials of Shengjing Board of Rites and Ceremonies began to worship spirit tablets and offer sacrifices.

隆恩殿前狮子／左页图
Stone Lion in Front of Eminent Favor Hall / Left Page
东配殿／上图
East Side-hall / Upper
[长23.44米，宽12.93米，高11.27米]
(23.44 meters long, 12.93 meters wide, 11.27 meters high)

西配殿 / 右页图
West Side-hall / Right Page
[长23.44米, 宽12.93米, 高11.27米]
(23.44 meters long, 12.93 meters wide, 11.27 meters high)

为喇嘛诵经建的西配殿

西配殿在隆恩殿西厢,共五间,建筑样式与东配殿相同,经我实测,面阔18米,进深7.95米。东西配殿,虽然建筑的风格极为一致,如歇山顶、面阔三间、进深两间、周围出廊等,但在功能上却是各有其用。努尔哈赤生前信奉喇嘛教,此殿的特殊用途是太祖和孝慈高皇后"忌辰"(去世之日)大祭时,即每年的八月十一日和孝慈高皇后的忌辰九月二十七日这两天福陵举行特祭的时候,西配殿将开启,作为喇嘛们诵经作法超度亡灵的地方。忌辰当日,盛京礼部要发布文告,官民人等需穿孝服,不许祭神、宴客、奏乐娱乐等,各衙门亦不能办理刑罚之类的公务。祭陵者更是要一身孝服参祭,届时众多的喇嘛就在西配殿诵经超度。

努尔哈赤生前信奉喇嘛教,皇太极时期为笼络蒙古更是不遗余力地推崇之,兴建的皇寺实胜寺等都是喇嘛教寺院,因而喇嘛诵经成为太祖及其皇后祭典中的一道特殊风景也不稀奇。西配殿内除陈设有条案等用具外,还相应地有喇嘛教的宗教用品唐卡、条桌、座具等陈设。女真族最原始的信仰是萨满教,后来随着政治与联姻的需要,信仰有所改变,信喇嘛教,有利于团结蒙古、青海、西藏等地。北京的雍和宫,原来是雍王府,即雍正皇帝登基前的家,乾隆帝在此出生。雍和宫在乾隆九年改为喇嘛庙,成为全国最高级别的佛教寺庙。而乾隆因为香妃的缘故,还在圆明园修建了清真寺。清朝历代皇室之所以都极力推崇佛教,也是为了国家一统的目的。

WEST SIDE-HALL BUILT FOR SUTRAS CHANTING

West Side-hall is in the west wing of Eminent Favor Hall with a total number of five bays and is of the same architectural style as East Side-hall. According to my site measurement, it is 18 meters wide and 7.95 meters deep. Although West Side-hall and East Side-hall are completely identical in the architectural style, such as hip-and-gable roof, three-bay width, two-bay depth and periphery projecting beyond the corridor, they have different functions. Nurhaci believed in Lamaism during his lifetime. The special purpose of West Side-hall was that at the time of big sacrifices for death days of Emperor Tai Tsu and Empress Xiaocigao, namely for the special sacrifices on August 11 and September 27 of each year, it would be opened for lamas to release souls of the dead from suffering by reciting scriptures and performing rituals. On anniversary of death date, Shengjing Board of Rites and Ceremonies issued a proclamation, specifying that praying to gods, entertaining and playing music for amusement were not allowed, nor could yamen handle official duties relating to penalties. Those sacrifice participants must wear mourning clothes while a number of lamas recited scriptures in West Side-hall.

Nurhaci believed in Lamaism during his lifetime and Hong Taiji spared no effort to advocate it to win Mongolia over; the imperial temples such as Shisheng Temple were all Lama temples. Therefore, it was not rare that lamas reciting scriptures became a special scene of the sacrifice for Emperor Tai Tsu and his empress. In addition to long narrow tables, West Side-hall was also provided with other relevant Lamaism items, such as Thangka, rectangle tables and chairs. The most primitive religion of Jurchen was Shamanism, and it was changed into Lamaism later for needs of politics and intermarriages, which was conducive to unite Mongolia, Qinghai and Tibet. Lama Temple in Beijing is originally Yong Mansion, and former residence of Emperor Yongzheng before his reign and also birth place of Emperor Qianlong. The Mansion was changed into Lama Temple in the 9th ruling year of Emperor Qianlong and became one of the country's highest level Buddhist temples. For the sake of Concubine Xiang, Qianlong also built a mosque in Summer Palace. The reason why emperors of Qing Dynasty highly honor Buddhism is clearly for national unity.

清东陵（裕陵）焚帛炉 / 左图
Silk-burning Pavilion in East Qing Mausoleum (Yu Mausoleum) / Left
焚帛炉 / 右图
Silk-burner / Right
春色焚帛炉 / 右页图
Silk-burner in Spring / Right Page

POST OFFICE BETWEEN LIFE AND DEATH — SILK-BURNING PAVILION

Standing in front of Eminent Favor Hall, watching the buildings inside Fuling Imperial Tomb, I can't help being overcome with nostalgic feelings for the past, especially when I am thinking of emperors' sacrificial offering to their ancestors. To the southwest corner of Eminent Favor Hall, there is a silk-burning pavilion, used for burning prayer tablets, silks, colorful papers, gold and silver foils (made of silk or papers) and other offerings in grand sacrifices of Qingming Festival, Ghost Festival, Winter Solstice and close of the year.

"There are a lot of graves on north and south hills, and many people are worshiping their ancestors in Qingming; ashes are flying like white butterflies, and blood tears dye azaleas red." Gao Juqing, a poet in South Song Dynasty once described tombs visiting activities in his poem "Qingming." In their Survey of Scenery in the Imperial Capital, Liu Tong and Yu Yizheng in Ming Dynasty wrote, "in Qingming Festival of lunar March, men and women are carrying pots, baskets, boxes and the like, with paper money on back of their horses and sedan chairs, to worship their ancestors. People kneel down before tomb to show respect, offer wines or remove grass, add soil on the tombs and burn ghost money or put them on top of the tomb. If there is tomb without any ghost money on it, then it must be tomb with nobody to worship. After that, they don't return yet; they find a place to inebriate themselves in order to forget sadness of remembering their beloved ones." These descriptions vividly depict the scenes how ancient people showed respects to their ancestors in Qingming Festival. Ordinary people lay so much emphasis on such activities, not to mention royal and noble families.

Silk-burning Pavilion is also known as "burning furnace," a small white marble-carved, hip-and-gable roof, pavilion-style building, with a full-height of 2.46 meters; its large ridge, vertical ridge, corrugated sheet, eave tile, beam ans bucket arch are all vividly of carved bluestone bricks and tiles and wooden structures. The furnace body is surrounded by screen-doors and four in each side (only two in its northern and western sides remain now with the other twelve lost). There is a round fire pool in the pavilion with a diameter of 0.7 meters, with wind holes on four directions. There is a coin-shaped vent on top of east and west gables. In accordance with grand sacrificial rituals, there should be ten thousand pieces of paper money and ten thousand golden and silver foils burnt for emperor and empress on grand sacrifices. One thousand pieces of paper money and one thousand pieces of golden and silver foils should be burnt for concubines and court ladies. One thousand pieces of plain paper and one thousand pieces of golden and silver foils should be burnt for call ladies, noble ladies and attendant ladies. It is the last procedure of grand sacrifices when Emperor watches the whole process of burning sacrificial offerings to show his filial piety during his eastern tour for worship, which is called "Burning Watch." The whole grand sacrifice ends in the dazzling smoke and fire of Silk-burning Pavilion, together with wailings of all participating officials and sutras chanting of the monks. This little pavilion is like a post office between life and death, delivering griefs and missings of the living to the deceased by burning such sacrificial offering as colorful papers, gold and silver foils.

As for this simple silk-burning pavilion, I have made comparisons with the other two, among which the pavilion in Yong Mausoleum is simply made of grey bricks with iron cast door; the one in Fuling Imperial Tomb is slightly different from that in Zhaoling Imperial Tomb in that Fuling Imperial Tomb's is relatively short and only half a Sumeru throne is left while the Sumeru throne in Zhaoling Imperial Tomb is complete. And also, buildings in Fuling Imperial Tomb are considerably short than those in Zhaoling Imperial Tomb, for absence of high foundation, as which I am puzzled. I always wonder if there might be something under Silk-burning Pavilion, part of which might be buried underground, but no one is willing to let me take a shovel to dig, so it becomes a mystery lingering in my mind. On May 20, 2011, an article of "Post Office Bridging Life and Death — Silk-burning Pavilion" was published in Shenyang Evening News. At half past eight of that same day, I dug a probe pit at the west side of Silk-burning Pavilion with the permission from Fuling Imperial Tomb Management Department, and I found a complete Sumeru throne and a large area of rammed earth layer. Near the base of the Sumeru throne there is covered with square grey bricks, from which I inferred that it was covered by later generations for tree planting.

Silk-burning Pavilions of Three Mausoleums outside Shanhai Pass are slightly different in name from those inside the Pass, which are called Silk-burning Stoves. Both the Pavilions and the Stoves have the same functions, but Silk-burning Stoves inside the Pass are more gorgeously decorated and delicate. Each Silk-burning Stove is of small glazed enclosed structure while Silk-burning Pavilion is a simple pavilion with four pillars, eaves and openings on its four sides.

人无路，魂有道的二柱门

隆恩殿后有一个"二柱门"，即棂星门，这也是清代陵制的特点之一，是以两根方形石柱形成的一间而构成了一个独立的硬山式建筑，夹山顶，两旁各有一根方形石柱，石柱高约8米，前后有抱鼓石，顶部有方形须弥座，座上有一"石吼"呈坐南朝北状。石柱间横以绘有和玺彩画的木额枋，额枋上下镶透空花板，门顶覆黄琉璃瓦，额枋下正中为对开合扇门，两旁实以木板。也可以这样说，棂星门是使用了木额枋的石牌楼，它的两根石柱出头且柱顶有望天吼，在对着大明楼的方向。而清东陵和清西陵则称为"蹲龙"，是面对面的。

此建筑虽名为门，平时不开启，只有在大祭之时才能洞开，实际上棺椁也不从此处过，谒陵者也不从此通行，只是祭陵时皇帝或主祭者献酒、举哀（哭陵）的地方，"人无路，魂有道"，二柱门是留给灵魂出入的地方，是纯礼制性的建筑，没有实用价值。很近道光帝慕陵以后开始不设置。而慕陵里不仅没有二柱门，神功圣德碑，月牙城等，甚至没有风水红墙，而是灰黄交融的墙垣，也没有宝城，可以说是清陵中规制较小却比较独特的陵寝。自道光帝之后，清帝的陵寝就都没有二柱门了。相比之下，关外三陵中，永陵没有也二柱门，而是直接在启运殿的北墙开了门洞，为灵魂直接出入的，而福陵，昭陵则都单独建有二柱门。

DUAL PILLAR DOOR WHERE SPIRIT ENTERS AND EXITS

Behind Eminent Favor Hall is Dual Pillar Door, also named Lingxing Gate, which is one feature of mausoleums in Qin Dynasty. A bay formed by two square stone pillars creates an independent flush gable-roof building. On either side is a square stone pillar with a height of 8 meters, with a bearing stone each behind and in front. On top of the pillar is a square Sumeru throne, on which there is a stone Sky Roaring Hou. Between two pillars is a horizontal tablet colorfully painted with Harmony seal on it. The lower and upper parts of the horizontal tablet are inlaid with open flower boards. The door is covered with yellow glazed tiles. Under the horizontal tablet are two split doors right in the middle with wooden boards seamed on both sides. In another word, Lingxing Gate is a stone memorial archway with a wooden horizontal tablet. Its two pillars are above the top with Sky Roaring Hous sitting on them toward Grand Ming Tower. But they are called as "squatting dragons" in East and West Qing Mausoleums, sitting there opposite.

Although defined as gate, this building is actually not open at normal times until at time of grand sacrifices. In fact, neither coffins nor mausoleum visitors pass through it. It is the place where Emperor or sacrifice officials offer wine, and mourn. The Gate, which is used for spirits to enter and exit, is a purely ritual building without any practical value. The Gate didn't stop existing until Emperor Daoguang's Mu Mausoleum, in which there were not built Dual Pillar Gate, Stele of Divine Merits, Crescent City, Burial Bastion, and even red geomantic walls (only grey yellowish walls), a small-scale but quite unique mausoleum. This kind of gate was forbidden for mausoleums since the time of Emperor Daoguang. In contrast, among Three Mausoleums outside the Pass, there isn't dual pillar gate either in Yong Mausoleum, but there are Luck-provoking Hall opened on its north wall for spirits to enter and exit. In Fu or Zhaoling Imperial Tomb, Dual Pillar Gate is erected respectively.

清西陵（泰陵）的二柱门／左上图、中上图
Dual Pillar Gate in West Qing Mausoleum (Tai Mausoleum) / Upper Left, Upper Middle
清西陵（崇陵）无二柱门／右上图
No Dual Pillar Gate in West Qing Mausoleum (Chong Mausoleum) / Upper Right
二柱门／右页图
Dual Pillar Gate / Right Page
［长7.98米，宽2.36米，高8.33米］
(7.98 meters long, 2.36 meters wide, 8.33 meters high)

皇帝举哀之处——石五供

通过隆恩门的门洞时，我总会感到阴森的凉气。即使夏天站在门洞下，依然感到寒气逼人。通过门洞，就可以看见，有一个石头做的祭台。为了祭典的需要，棂星门后有一长条石案，这就是石祭台。祭台为汉白玉雕刻，须弥座式，上枋刻有缠枝莲及宝相花，台上正中为一石鼎炉，此炉也称"海山"，由内到外依次是一对石花瓶和一对石烛台，人们又称它为"石五供"。只有道光帝慕陵内的石五供由内到外依次是香炉、石蜡台和石花瓶。炉中立有"紫石火焰"，石花瓶上也立有紫石，取香烟不断，烛火长明，大清江山万代之意。福陵石花瓶和石烛台上的事物已经丢失了，昭陵石花瓶上的两块紫石尚存。由此我不由想到了李白的诗句"日照香炉生紫烟"，诗中提到的"紫烟"并不是紫色的烟，而是象征着紫气东来的祥瑞之气，与石五供上的紫石寓意暗合。石五供对民国时期总统的陵寝建筑有着很深的影响，不论是袁世凯墓、还是张作霖的元帅林都有石五供，只是元帅林内没有石祭台，把石五供直接放在了地面上。

石祭台可以说是石雕题材和内容最丰富的艺术作品，鼎炉的炉盖雕正龙，石座上雕有"佛八宝"（注解22）和"暗八仙"（注解23），除了这样的道教纹饰，还有含有象征意义的吉祥图案，如柿子、如意（事事如意），净瓶、鹌鹑（平平安安）等，所有这一切，都是为了表达祝愿太祖高皇帝和孝慈高皇后吉祥的目的。皇帝东巡祭祖时在石祭台前"献祭"和"举哀"以表其孝心和"瞻恋"之诚。我不明白的是，为什么殿里有供桌，这里还要再单独设置一个石头的供桌。为什么永陵中没有设置石五供，福陵昭陵中却都设置了？

福陵和昭陵内隆恩殿、二柱门、石五供距离很近，近到行人都无法通行的地步。而清东陵、清西陵三者之间的距离要远得多，在隆恩殿后面还有陵寝门，是三座琉璃花门，它们是整个陵寝前朝和后寝的分界线。

石五供海山／左页图
Haishan (Furnace) of Stone Five Offerings／Left Page

二柱门／上图
Dual Pillar Gate／Upper

EMPEROR MOURNING PLACE — STONE FIVE OFFERINGS

I always feel gruesome cool air when passing through Eminent Favor Gate. Even if standing under the door in summer, I can still feel its chill. Upon entering the gate, one can see a stone altar. This long stone table is provided for sacrificial ceremonies behind Lingxing Gate. It is of Sumeru-throne type carved from white marble, the upper beam of which bears carvings of winding lotus pattern and composite flowers. A stone tripod furnace, also called "Haishan" (meaning "seamount") is built in the middle of altar, furnished symmetrically with stone candlestick holders and stone incense vases, which people call Stone Five Offerings. Only in Mu Mausoleum of Emperor Daoguang are Stone Five Offerings arranged in the sequence of incense furnace, stone incense holders and stone incense vases from inside to outside. In the furnace, there are "purple stone flames," and on top of the stone vases, implying continuous burning of joss sticks and candles, and blessing for the territory of Qing Dynasty. The items on the stone holders and vases in Fuling Imperial Tomb have been lost, while purple stones on the vases remain in Zhaoling Imperial Tomb, from which I could not help thinking of Li Bai's poem "The sunlit censer exhales a wreath of purple mist", "Zi Yan" (purple mist) here doesn't refer to purple mist, but a symbol of good fortune, which matches the implied meaning of purple stones on Stone Five Offerings. Stone Five Offerings also have deep influence on Presidents' mausoleum construction in the Republican Period; Stone Five Offerings can be found in both Yuan Shikai's tomb and

石五供
Stone Five Offerings

Marshal Zhang Zuolin's woods; one difference is that in Zhang's Tomb, no stone altar was built and Stone Five Offerings were directly placed on the ground.

These sacrificial items symbolize long burning of joss sticks and candles. The stone altar is an art piece that has the richest stone carvings. Dragon is carved on cover of furnace while "Eight Buddhist emblems" (Note 22) and "Covert Eight Immortals" (Note 23) are carved on the stone base. In addition to these Taoist ornaments, there are also symbolic auspicious patterns, e.g. shizi (persimmons), ruyi (which can be combined to mean that everything goes well), and water bottle and quail (meaning safe and sound), all of which are meant to wish Emperor Tai Tsu and Empress Xiaocigao propitious. On royal eastward tour for ancestor worship, emperors offer sacrifices and mourn before this stone altar to express filial piety and sincere admiration. This extra stone altar puzzles me considering the existence of an incense burner for sacrifices inside Eminent Favor Hall. And I am still not clear why both Zhaoling Imperial Tomb and Fuling Imperial Tomb have Stone Five Offerings while Yong Mausoleum doesn't have.

In Fu or Zhaoling Imperial Tomb, the distances between Eminent Favor Hall, Double Pillar Gate and Stone Five Offerings are too close for people to pass through. But the distances between these three buildings inside East or West Qing Mausoleum are much farther. And in the back of Eminent Favor Hall, there are also mausoleum gates, which are three color-glazed gates, a boundary line of the entire mausoleum's front and rear parts.

大明楼／左图
Grand Ming Tower / Left
[长10.06米，宽10.06米，高11.43米]
(10.06 meters long, 10.06 meters wide, 11.43 meters high)

雷火中永生的大明楼

洞门之上的红楼就是大明楼，也叫"明楼"，康熙四年三月（1665年）建造，它位于方城正北的城台之上，与隆恩门楼遥遥相对，矗立在方城的尽头，它也是福陵内的最高建筑物。在建筑布局上，福陵陵园实在需要有一座屏障作为背景，作为所有建筑的一个强有力的收束。大明楼重檐九脊方形碑楼式建筑，黄琉璃瓦顶，梁柱天花施以彩画，各有拱形券门，下部是方形台基。屋檐的正面悬挂门额，门额上刻有满蒙汉三种文字的"福陵"二字，我一直不解的是，为什么要把福陵的匾额悬挂在这里？因其最高，还是起着提示人们即将看到太祖的宝城地宫的作用，也或者是因为这里供着福陵圣号碑？

大明楼，实际上是建在方城上的又一座碑楼，它的建筑形制与神功圣德碑楼相同，只是在建筑体量上更显高大雄伟。大明楼内的正中也竖立着一甬石碑，碑首雕龙，碑额是"大清"篆字，碑身正面满文居中，蒙汉各居左右地题写着"太祖高皇帝之陵"几个大字，是为努尔哈赤的庙号和谥号碑。庙号是皇帝死后，被立室奉祀时所赐予的名号，形式多是表示为某祖某宗，如太祖、太宗。谥号是皇帝、后妃、王公、大臣、贵族及士大夫死后，根据他们生前的品行和事迹，给他们评定的称号，是对这个人一生浓缩了的评价。

福陵中的匾额一般都将满文居中，将汉文安排在左侧，强调满文的重要地位，大明楼内的太祖谥号碑上的文字排列顺序也是如此，这大概是清入关后强调"国语骑射（注解24）"而在建筑上的一种反映吧。长久以来，女真人只有语言而没有文字，一直到努尔哈赤时，仍然是借用蒙文和汉文。女真人讲女真语，写蒙古文，这十分不利于政令的通行，政权建立之后，努尔哈赤的内外联系更为频繁，没有自己的文字，认识蒙文的人又不多，使得上下难于沟通，严重地阻碍了新政权的发展。因此，努尔哈赤决心创制满族自己的文字。遵照努尔哈赤的旨

大明楼 / 右图
Grand Ming Tower / Right

意, 额尔德尼、噶盖二位大臣, 根据本民族语言的特点, 仿照蒙古文字母, 创制了满文, 即所谓"老满文, 或无圈点满文"。这是满族文化史上的一件大事, 它促进了满族社会的进步, 扩大了与相邻民族的交往, 并为后来女真人的全面统一, 建立"后金"政权, 以至入主中原起到了非常重要的作用。到皇太极时, 满文得到进一步改进与完善。而满文和满语对整个中华民族的影响, 都是巨大的, 其实我们今天说的普通话就是源于满人入关后为了与汉族人交流而创立的普通话。民国时, 满语成了国语, 到了新中国就成了普通话,"普通话"一词的英语单词是"mandarin"就是"满族人发明的话"的意思。今天的北京被视为东北方言的语言岛, 北京话被视为标准普通话, 而在清之前, 全国普遍流行的普通话则类似于今天广东客家话, 因为我国南方基本完整保存了古汉语的发音。现在的日语和朝鲜语中的发音和我国南方的古汉语发音有系统性的相似, 原因就是日本和朝鲜古代的时候向中国学习文化, 他们现在的文字读音和中国古代的文字读音相似, 而与400年前才出现的普通话则离得较远。

大明楼内的石碑即为福陵圣号碑, 碑身四边刻有游龙为饰。碑座为须弥式。上枋南北面刻二龙戏珠, 东西各刻火焰珠和单行龙。据说, 圣号碑碑文应由嗣皇帝书写, 因为福陵圣号碑立于康熙三年五月(1664年), 此碑应该是康熙皇帝手书真迹。"圣号碑"地位特殊, 碑面用朱砂染成红色, 碑文填金, 其他各部用红、黄、白、兰、绿五色彩绘, 金光闪闪, 鲜艳夺目。清末以后, 碑由于年久失修而色彩脱落。1962年5月7日, 大明楼因雷火被毁, 此碑受到一定损坏。六十年代, 三年自然灾害, 国家民族多灾多难, 人民生灵涂炭, 处于水深火热中, 福陵没有受到妥善保护, 也是正常的。福陵中隆恩殿中所供的神牌,"太祖"立祖而居于正中, 后嗣皇帝按辈分高低再依左(称为昭)右(称为穆)顺序排列, 努尔哈赤当仁不让地成为清朝太祖, 他这一庙号被刻于牌位之上, 举行了升祔太庙礼后, 永为其后代供奉尊崇。因努尔哈赤的庙号谥号全称是"太祖承天广运圣德神功肇纪立极仁孝睿武端毅钦安弘文定业高皇帝", 所以大明楼圣号碑上刻有"太祖高皇帝"几个字。大明楼命运坎坷, 现在的大明楼是20世纪80年代修复的建筑风貌。

大明楼石碑／左页图
Stele of Grand Ming Tower / Left Page
大明楼石碑火灾后、修复后旧照对比／上图
Contrast of Pictures of Burned and Renovated Grand Ming Tower / Upper

GRAND MING TOWER, SURVIVAL FROM THUNDER AND LIGHTNING

The red building on top of the funnel is Grand Ming Tower, also called "Ming Tower." It was built in March of the 4th ruling year of Emperor Kang Xi (1665), located on top of the wall platform in the north of Square City, standing far away opposite to Eminent Favor Hall. It stands tall and upright at the end of Square City. In layout, Fuling Imperial Tomb needs a screen as its background, thus bringing together everything in the building into an integrated closure. Ming Tower is a square stele pavilion of double eave and nine-ridged purlin, and with yellow glazed tiles on its roof. Its ceiling, beams and columns are colored with paintings. The Tower stands on a square platform, with four arched doors on four sides. A horizontal tablet is suspended under the front eave, inscribed with "Fuling Imperial Tomb" in Manchu, Mongolian and Chinese. I have been confused all the time why they set a horizontal tablet here. Is it because it is the highest point of the building, or because it reminds people that they are going to see the underground palace of Treasure City, or because the Imperial Tombstone of Fuling Imperial Tomb is enshrined here?

Grand Ming Tower, in fact, is another stele pavilion built on Square Cty, whose building system and form conform to those of Stele of Divine Merits, but more magnificent and spectacular in architectural form. In the center of Ming Tower, there stands a stone tablet, with its head carved with dragon, and the top part with characters "大清" (Great Qing) in seal script. The tablet body is inscribed with "Mausoleum of Emperor Tai Tsu," with Manchu characters in the middle, and Mongolian and Chinese on its left and right respectively, which is tablet of the posthumous title of Emperor Nurhaci. Temple name is the title offered in receiving the enshrinement after an emperor's death, which is mostly expressed as × Tsu and × Zong, such as Tai Tsu and Tai Zong. Posthumous title is the title offered by appraising their lifelong conducts and deeds after the death of Emperor, Empress, nobility, ministers, aristocrats and literati, which is the condensed evaluation of this person's whole life.

Generally, the Manchu characters are in the middle and Chinese characters on the left to show Manchu's importance. The order of characters on such tablets for emperors' posthumous titles are generally alike, which may be a reflection of the policy of emphasizing "National Language and Riding-Shooting" (Note 24) after Qing people entered Shanhai Pass. For a long time, Jurchen's language had no writing; they were still using Mongolian and Chinese till Nurhaci. They spoke in Jurchen language but wrote in Mongolian, which was not conducive to passage of decrees; after establishment of their regime, Nurhaci had more frequent internal and external contacts; without their own writing, it was very hard to communicate, which seriously impeded development of the new regime.

Therefore, Nurhaci determined to create his own Manchu written language. In accordance with orders of Nurhaci, two ministers Erdeni and Gegai, created Manchu writing, the so-called "old Manchu writing or non-punctuated Manchu writing" according to characteristics of the their ethnical language and Mongolian alphabet. It is a major event in the history of Manchu culture, which promoted progresses of Manchu society and expanded communication with neighboring ethnics; it also played a very important role in the later full reunification of Jurchen, the establishment of "Later Jin" regime and the entry to Central Plains. At the time of Hong Taiji, Manchu writing had been further improved and perfected. The influence of Manchu writing and Manchu language on the entire Chinese nation is significant; in fact, Standard Chinese we speak today is from Mandarin, which is created to communicate with Han people by Manchu after their entry. During Republic of China, Manchu became the national language, and became Standard Chinese in new China. The English word "Standard Chinese" is from "Mandarin," which means "the language invented by Manchu." Today's Beijing is considered a language island of the northeast dialect, and Beijing dialect is considered Standard Chinese; but before Qing Dynasty, the generally popular Standard Chinese in our country is similar to today's Hakka in Guangdong Province, for the southern China basically keeps the intact ancient Chinese pronunciation. Now Japanese and Korean pronunciations are systematically similar to ancient Chinese pronunciation of southern China and the reason is that ancient Japan and Korea learned cultures from China; pronunciations of their current writings are similar to that of ancient Chinese, but are far away from Mandarin which appeared 400 years ago.

Stone tablet inside Grand Ming Tower is Imperial Title Tablet of Fuling Imperial Tomb, the four sides of which are inscribed with flying dragons, and the foundation of which is of Sumeru throne type. Southern and northern parts of its upper pillar are inscribed with "Two Dragon Playing with a Pearl" and its western and eastern parts are single dragon and flaming orb. It is said that inscriptions on Imperial Title Tablet was handwriting of succeeding Emperor. As Imperial Title Tablet was established in May, the 3rd ruling year of Emperor Kangxi (1664), it should be the authentic handwriting of Emperor Kang Xi. Due to its special status, Imperial Title Tablet is dyed into red with cinnabar, its inscription is filled with gold, and other parts are painted with red, yellow, white, blue and green colors, shining with glow. From late Qing Dynasty on, paints on the Tablet have been shed due to lack of maintenance. In 1962, Grand Ming Tower was burned up due to thunder and lightning, and its Tablet was partially destroyed. In the 1960s, during three years' natural calamity of China, the entire nation was facing fierce disasters and the people were in an abyss of misery, so it is normal that Fuling Imperial Tomb was not under proper protection. Among spirit tablets enshrined in Hall of Eminent Favor in Fuling Imperial Tomb, the tablet of Nurhaci is placed in the middle and the succeeding emperors are so arranged in order according to their seniorities in the clan with left position is called "昭" (bright) and right position, "穆" (solemn). As the founding father of Qing Dynasty, Nurhaci was naturally regarded as Tai Tsu and his temple name was inscribed on the tablet. He was respected and worshiped after the ceremony of placing him in the royal temple. As the full posthumous title of Nurhaci is "Tai Tsu, divine, fortunate, virtuous, great, inchoate, mighty, filial, wise, firm, lateral and devoted emperor." Therefore, Imperial Title Tablet of Ming Tower is inscribed with "Emperor Tai Tsu." After these ups and downs, Ming Tower was renovated in 1980s with new architectural features.

大明楼火灾后与复建后对比 / 下图
Contrast of Burned and Renovated Grand Ming Tower / Lower
大明楼 / 右页图
Grand Ming Tower / Right Page

清东陵（裕陵）月牙城／上图
Crescent City of East Qing Mausoleum (Yu Mausoleum) / Upper
月牙城／右页图
Crescent City / Right Page

月牙城还是哑巴院？

方城后是月牙城，因形状如同一弯新月而得名。月牙城是方城和半圆形宝城之间出现的一个特殊空间，并在此修建了"蹬道"，以上下方城和宝城。月牙城在民间也被称为哑巴城或者哑巴院，关于这个还有一个未解的谜。据说地宫建成后，怕工匠泄露秘密，官府将所有工匠集中在月牙城，用药将人全部毒哑了，因此得名哑巴院。也有一种说法是说，修地宫时，招来的所有工匠就是根本不会说话的哑巴。不管事实究竟如何，这都是历史留给我们无法解答的疑问了。如果说将工匠毒哑不人道，但比起以前已经有很大进步了，因为清朝已经不采用将工匠殉葬这种残酷的方式了。月牙城这种建筑形式，在明代及其以前的陵寝中是没有的。每一个时期的建筑，都有它的沿袭性和创造性，月牙城就是属于清朝的创造性产物吧。古语云："人有悲欢离合，月有阴晴圆缺"以月牙则代表离散，人死谓之亏，修成月牙形，暗喻悲哀吧。清代陵寝中，关内陵寝一般都有月牙城和宝城除了道光帝的慕陵，与关外三陵不同的是，关内陵寝的宝城一般都是整圆形，月牙向内，而关外宝城却是半圆形，月牙向外，永陵宝城特殊点，呈八角弧形。

CRESCENT CITY OR DUMB'S COURTYARD

Crescent City lies behind Square City, which gains its name from its crescent shape. Crescent City is a special courtyard between Square City and a semi-circular Burial Bastion with a flight of steps built for easy access. According to folk stories, Crescent City is also called Dumb's City or Dumb's Courtyard, whose origin remains an enigma. It is said when the underground palace was completed, all craftsmen were poisoned dumb in crescent city to prevent them from disclosing the secrets of the underground palace, hence the name. Another story goes like this: all the workers recruited were dumbs. Whatever the truth it is, it is a riddle unsolved. Although it was inhuman to poison craftsman dumb, it was still a progress compared with previous dynasties, as Qing Dynasty gave up burying alive with the dead. There weren't crescent cities in mausoleums before Qing Dynasties. Buildings in every period have its inheritance and creativity, and Crescent City is a unique architectural form of Qing Dynasty. As a poem goes, "People may have sorrow or joy, be near or far apart; the moon may be dim or bright, wax or wane," so a crescent moon is usually used to represent separation. Thus the death of a person correlates with the waning of a moon, and the building is built in the form of a crescent moon in order to signify sadness. Of the mausoleums of Qing Dynasty inside the Shanhai Pass, there are Crescent Cities and Burial Bastions above the underground palace, but Mu Mausoleum of Daoguang Emperor is an exception. Burial Bastions inside the Pass are usually round-shaped with inward Crescents. In contrast, Burial Bastions outside the Pass are semicircled with outward crescents. And what is typical the Bastion in Yong Mausoleum is its octagonal shape.

福陵月牙城 / 左页图
Crescent City of Fuling Imperial Tomb / Left Page
清西陵（泰陵）月牙城 / 左上图
Crescent City of West Qing Mausoleum (Tai Mausoleum) / Upper Left
清东陵（裕陵）月牙城 / 右上图、左下图
Crescent City of East Qing Mausoleum (Yu Mausoleum) / Upper Right, Lower Left
清西陵（崇陵）月牙城 / 右下图
Crescent City in West Qing Mausoleum (Chong Mausoleum) / Lower Right

十一与福陵风水

月牙城内空旷、沉寂，气氛压抑，只有北墙正中镶嵌着一座彩色琉璃照壁，又叫"月牙影壁"。影壁上的琉璃有系着绿色彩带的花瓶图案，瓶中生长着象征富贵的枝叶繁茂的牡丹花。据说五光十色的牡丹花中暗藏着开启地宫的机关，也是地宫的入口。福陵影壁墙上的牡丹有11朵，很多人都推测这11朵花的含义，甚至揣测到昭陵的影壁墙上12朵牡丹，是寓意大清帝国的十二位君主。我个人研究分析后，认为福陵的11朵牡丹，并非世人所猜测的那样神秘，寓意大清的命运的君主之类，因为11这个数字，对努尔哈赤来说，意义非常独特，甚至关系着他一生的命运。我可以列举几个数字，努尔哈赤是万历十一年起兵反明的，天命十一年他故去，故去的时间是天命十一年8月11日，而他的陵寝，福陵又坐落在沈阳市东北天柱山上11公里处，甚至在他攻打宁远城的时候，袁崇焕是在宁远城上架设了11门红衣大炮将他打败的。而据史料记载，努尔哈赤除大妃富察氏、孟古姐姐、阿巴亥外，还有11名庶妃。按理这些庶妃都应葬入福陵妃园寝，可是据文献记载，妃园寝中只葬了3个妃子。其余8个妃子葬在哪里？由于史料的缺失，成了难解的谜。而福陵影壁墙上的11朵牡丹，究竟是有所寓意，还是巧合？与此类似的是昭陵的影壁墙上有12朵牡丹，而关于这12与大清的关系，就有了更多的臆想与猜测，故事就更多了。这11与12之间，还有关内其他清代陵寝影壁上的牡丹数，究竟暗含着怎样的历史谜题，后人不过是臆测，真正确的答案恐怕只有当时的设计者才能给出吧。

地宫影壁／上图
Screen Wall of Underground Palace／Upper
[长5.72米，高4.9米]
(5.72 meters long, 4.9 meters high)
大明楼楼下通往月牙城的门洞／下图
Archway Beneath Grand Ming Tower Leading to Crescent City／Lower
影壁上的牡丹／右页图
Peonies on Screen Wall of Underground Palace／Right Page

NUMBER 11 AND GEOMANCY OF FULING IMPERIAL TOMB

Inside Crescent City, it is open, quiet, and its atmosphere is depressing. There is a glazed screen wall embedded in the middle of the north wall, which is also called "Crescent Screen Wall." There is a flower bottle on the screen wall, with green ribbons tied to it, and peonies in the bottle signify wealth and dignity. It is said that among these gorgeous peonies there hides a mechanism which can open the door to the underground palace, where also serves as entrance to the palace. There are 11 peonies on the screen wall of Fuling Imperial Tomb. A lot of people are inferring the implications of the 11 flowers. Some even relate the 12 peonies to the 12 emperors of Great Qing Dynasty. According to my own study and analysis, I don't think there is any interrelationship between peonies and emperors and fate of Qing Dynasty. Actually, the number is significantly related to the fate of Nurhaci. I can list a few events related to the number of 11. For example, Nurhaci rose up in the 11th ruling year of Emperor Wanli against Ming Dynasty and died on August 11 of the 11th ruling year of Tianming. His mausoleum, Fuling Imperial Tomb, lies in 11 kilometers of Mount Tianzhu, northeast of Shenyang city. He was defeated by Yuan Chonghuan with 11 cannons when he tried to seize Ningyuan City. According to historical records, Nurhaci has 11 additional concubines except for Fucha, Menggu Sister and Abahai. These concubines should have been buried in Fuling Imperial Tomb according to Qing regulations; however, only three concubines were buried in Noble Concubines Garden. Where are the other eight concubines? It remains an enigma due to lack of historical records. Is it an implication or coincidence? Similarly, there are 12 peonies on the screen wall of Zhaoling Imperial Tomb, which triggers more suppositions and conjectures over the number 12 and its relation with Qing Dynasty. However, what on earth are the puzzles of the number 11 and 12 and some other numbers of the peonies on the mausoleums inside the Pass? Maybe only the designers knew the exact answers.

宝顶里葬有几位妃子？

月牙城以北便是宝城，这是一座半圆形的"城"，又叫"团城"，由青砖垒砌，上顶外有雉堞，内有女墙，马道向外倾斜，与方城马道倾斜方向相反，并有排除积水的"荷叶沟"。相传修宝城要用"童子夯"，就是修夯打衬土时，用十岁左右的男童踩踏，不用木夯或石夯。因为在古代人心中，童男童女是圣洁、吉祥的象征。宝城中间是一座高大的圆丘，叫"宝顶"，又叫"独龙阜"，实为坟丘，是用三合土（白灰、黄土、砂子）掺和堆筑，要层层夯实，并进行五次"盘踩"。每次盘踩要在三合上中掺糯米汤，米汤黏稠，冷却之后坚固，最后在宝鼎外皮还要抹一层厚厚的白灰，使表面光洁，免受雨水渗透、冲刷。关外三陵比较，永陵宝顶在山坡底下，在启运山脚下，且数量达五个之多。而福陵、昭陵都只有一个宝顶，福陵宝顶在山上，而昭陵宝顶则建在平原上。

"宝顶"之下就是福陵的"心脏"部位——地宫。努尔哈赤与他的妻子们就长眠在这里。根据清初火葬的风俗习惯推测，福陵内埋葬的应是太祖的骨灰。清初满族的葬俗大都沿袭女真族的火葬习俗。雍正皇帝说："本朝肇迹关东，以师兵为护卫，迁徙无常。遇父母之丧，弃之不忍，携之不能，故用火化。"（《清高宗实录》卷五）所以，清初大都实行火葬。努尔哈赤时代，"死则翌日举之于野而焚之"（李民寔：《建州闻见录》）。入关后，只有顺治帝是火葬，因为受汉族文化影响，汉族实行土葬，无法接受火葬，故从康熙帝开始，就改行土葬了，并将此葬俗列入国法，即"一概不许火化，倘有犯者，按律治罪"（《清高宗实录》卷五），对先朝皇帝之词，也多加隐讳。直到新中国成立后，人们才重新认识到火葬的先进，其不知清朝在几百年前早就实行火葬了。

相关史料记载，福陵整个地宫建于康熙二年至六年之间（1663—1666年）。说起地宫，人们往往有神秘莫测之感，因为福陵的地宫从未开启过。不过从明十三陵及清乾隆、慈禧等陵寝的结构，可以大致推测出福陵地宫的结构。地宫入口应在陵的正前方，是一条坡形甬道，甬道尽头是由九券、四门组成的"主"字形地宫，最里边的券堂叫"金券"，是主要墓室，内有石床，帝后棺椁全部摆在石床之上，正当中是皇帝梓棺、梓棺之下有"金井"一眼，相传里边波涛汹涌，直通大海。这就是人们常说的"金井御葬"。不过，从已经出土的金井看，它不过是直径十厘米深不足尺的孔洞，"井内"葬有皇帝、皇后一些珍宝。实际上，金井只是地宫定位的水准点，是风水先生选陵址时定的穴位，并没有什么神秘之处可言。地宫内部，一般四壁都刻有精美的壁画，有随葬品，并有几层厚重的石门、每层门用"自来石"（注解25）封闭，十分坚固，正所谓，"一石当关，万夫莫开"。史料记载，努尔哈赤一共有十六位妃子，而大妃四位（包括后被追封的孟古），那么地宫里应至少葬有努尔哈赤和三位妃子的骨灰，因为第二位大妃富察氏获罪死，因而没有资格葬在福陵。那么孟古死时还有四位婢女陪葬，她们的骨灰是否也一起迁入福陵地宫？加上阿巴亥，一共九个人。这个数字和福陵管理人所说相符。但是，也有史料记载，和阿巴亥一起殉葬的还有两位素妃，那么她们的骨灰葬在哪里呢？福陵地宫究竟葬有多少人，恐怕只有上天知道了。

宝顶石门／上图
Stone Door of Blessed Vault／Upper

宝城／右页图
Burial Bastion／Right Page

HOW MANY CONCUBINES WERE BURIED IN BLESSED VAULT?

To the north of Crescent City, there is Burial Bastion. It is a semicircular "Bastion," also called "Round Bastion," built with black bricks. Zhidies, the battlements, are on the exterior side of burial bastion and parapet walls are inside the burial bastion. The riding track tilts to the outside, with the direction just opposite to that of Square City. Also, there is a lotus leaf shaped drainage system on the ground. It is said that Burial Bastion was rammered by 10-year-old boys treading on it instead of using wood or stone rammer, which is called "Boys' Rammering." In the minds of ancient people, young boys and girls are symbols of purity and auspiciousness. At the center of Burial Bastion, there is a high circular mound, actually a tomb, which is called "Blessed Vault," or "Single Dragon Mound." In fact, it is a mound solidly rammered with triple-combined soil (lime, sand and loess). It takes five rounds of rammerings layer by layer, in each of which the triple-combined soil should be blended with sticky rice soup. Finally, a layer of lime is pasted on the outside surface of Burial Bastion. Thus, its surface remains smooth and free from weathering. The treasure vaults of Yong Mausoleum are located at the foot of Mountain of Qiyun (Provoking Luck), with a total number of five. There is only one vault respectively in Fuling Imperial Tomb and Zhaoling Imperial Tomb. Blessed Vault of Fuling Imperial Tomb is on the top of a hill while that of Zhaoling Imperial Tomb is on a plain.

Under Blessed Vault is the heart of Fuling Imperial Tomb– the underground palace. Nurhaci and his wives are sleeping here permanently. According to cremating customs of Qing, what is buried inside Fuling Imperial Tomb must be cremains of Nurhaci. At the beginning of Qing Dynasty, Manchu's burial system conformed to that of Jurchen. As Emperor Yongzheng said, "great Qing came from east of Shanhai Pass and our army and people often moved around without a fixed residence. In case their parents died, they couldn't bear to desert their bodies and it was impossible to carry them along; therefore, cremation was adopted." (Records of Emperor Hong Taiji, Volume 5). So cremation was the norm at its beginning. According to Li Minshi's Records of Things Seen and Heard in Jianzhou, in times of Nurhaci, "when people die, their bodies are carried to the wild and burned the next day." After their entrance to southern part of Shanhai Pass, only Shun Zhi was cremated. Traditional Chinese culture couldn't bear the practice of cremation, and so from Emperor Kang Xi, cremation was replaced by inhumation. "Cremation is forbidden; whoever violates will be punished according to the law." (Records of Emperor Hong Taiji, Volume 5) So later generation emperors seldom mentioned the cremation practice set up by their ancestors. Until after foundation of People's Republic of China, people began to realize the advancement of cremation again, but few people know that it was once very popular several hundred years ago.

According to historical records, the entire underground palace of Fuling Imperial Tomb was built between the 2nd and 6th ruling year of Emperor Kangxi (from 1663 to 1666). Talking about the palace, people often feel it mysterious as it has never been opened. However, from the structures of Ming Tombs and mausoleums of Emperor Qianlong and Empress Dowager Cixi, we can infer somethiong about the structure of the underground palace of Fuling Imperial Tomb. The entrance of underground palace should be in the right front of the mausoleum, which leads to "主" -shaped underground palace composed of 9 arches and four doors. The innermost arch hall is called "Golden Arch" , which is a main coffin chamber. There is a stone bed inside on which all coffins of Emperor and Empress are placed. The one in the middle is Emperor's coffin, under which there is a "Gold Well." As legends go, there are tides and waves in the well which leads to the sea, which is therefore called "Gold Well Royal Burial." However, according to the unearthened mausoleums, the golden well is just a shallow hole less than 10 centimeters in diameter. Inside the well, there are a lot of treasures. In fact, gold well is only the bench mark to locate the underground palace, or a burial point selected by geomancer. It remains nothing mysterious. Inside the underground palace, generally speaking, there are beautiful murals on its four walls, and burial gifts with several stone gates installed and locked with "Auto-sliding Stone," (Note 25) which is very firm and tight. In one word, "One stone can hold the pass to guard against ten thousand enemies." According to historical records, Nurhaci has totally sixteen imperial concubines and four queens (including the later bestowed Menggu), then there should be at least ashes of Nurhaci and three concubines buried in this underground palace; the second queen Fucha was convicted, therefore she was not eligible for burial in Fuling Imperial Tomb. There were four maids buried for companionship when Menggu died, and were their ashes also moved into the underground palace of Fuling Imperial Tomb? Including Abahai, there are nine in total. This figure matches the number told by Manager of Fuling Imperial Tomb. However, according to other historical records, there are another two concubines buried alive together with Abahai, then where were their ashes buried? How many people are buried in the underground palace of Fuling Imperial Tomb, I am afraid only God knows that.

大妃阿巴亥是自愿殉葬吗？

其实福陵里，还葬有一位妃子，那就是大妃阿巴亥。关于努尔哈赤的感情，也一直是个谜，有人说努尔哈赤对孟古一往情深，也有人说孟古因为失意抑郁而死。我分析以后认为，后者的可能性更大些。因为从孟古嫁给努尔哈赤的时间看，她比努尔哈赤另一位受宠的妃子阿巴亥要早，但是当努尔哈赤的第二位妻子富察氏死后，被升为大妃的却是阿巴亥而不是孟古，孟古死后也没有被努尔哈赤追封。而孟古一生只生有皇太极一个孩子，阿巴亥却生有三个孩子，长子阿济格、次子多尔衮、三子多铎。从这些事实分析，孟古不一定是最受宠的那个妃子。相反，阿巴亥却是努尔哈赤临终前唯一要见的妃子。"母以子贵"当时登上皇位的如果是阿巴亥的儿子多尔衮的话，可能福陵的女主人就会是另一个人了。

阿巴亥，乌喇纳拉氏，生于明万历十七年（1589年），出身于乌喇部贵族，其父满泰，为海西乌喇部酋长。我曾在吉林市讲学，乌喇街的领导专门四次请我去考察。阿巴亥的部族先于孟古的部族六年，被丈夫努尔哈赤的部族建州女真所灭。

明万历二十九年（1601年），当时年仅12岁的阿巴亥，就嫁给努尔哈赤为侧福晋，成为努尔哈赤的第十位妻子。天命五年（1620年）即19岁时升为大妃，开始主持家政，她所生的3个儿子年龄虽小，但努尔哈赤却让他们每人掌握一个整旗。当时作为后金的根本，八旗军队只有8个旗，他们就占去3个，可见努尔哈赤对阿巴亥的情意所在。

努尔哈赤在天命十一年七月二十三日前往清河汤泉沐浴疗养，八月初七日，努尔哈赤病危，他一边乘船顺太子河返回沈阳，一边急召大妃阿巴亥来相见，大妃是见到了，但为时已晚，此时的努尔哈赤已经不能言语。

史学界一直认为，努尔哈赤去世后，诸王强迫阿巴亥殉葬，阿巴亥成为宫廷斗争的牺牲品。在努尔哈赤死前的4天中，唯有大妃阿巴亥承命侍侧。因此对于皇太极、代善等竞争势力来说，她是最致命的对手。若不将她铲除，她可借"遗命"之威，使自己的儿子登上汗位，尽管那可能是努尔哈赤的原意。但是，对于皇太极，他比当时年幼的多尔衮更成熟，也更深谙和掌握政治局势，他联合诸王捏造汗父"遗言"，迫令阿巴亥随殉。当时的满族还有生殉这种制度，生殉在封建社会也并不稀奇，但却是有条件的，作为生殉的妻妾，无幼子需要照顾且多为地位较低的妾。当时多尔衮和多铎年纪尚幼，大妃地位最尊，生殉怎么也不该轮到阿巴亥才对。当时的多尔衮虽然年幼，但对这一切却不可能不了解。阿巴亥会不会是自愿殉葬呢？

如果真如史学家分析的那样，阿巴亥殉葬前就没有给自己的儿子留下遗言吗？多尔衮和多铎后来手握重兵，为什么还要帮让自己生母殉葬的哥哥皇太极打江山呢？为什么还要帮皇太极的幼子福临坐稳江山呢？有人说，多尔衮没有篡顺治的位，是由于庄妃下嫁的缘故，现在已经证明纯属虚构的野史。

顺治七年（1650年），阿巴亥获得了"孝烈恭敏献哲仁和赞天俪圣武皇后"的谥号，其牌位也被供奉于太庙享受子孙的祭祀。多尔衮死后获罪，顺治帝还曾将多尔衮挫骨扬灰，但绝不敢冒天下之大不韪而擅动太祖之陵。因此，阿巴亥就一直默默无闻地陪伴汗夫而葬福陵了，只是她是否知道自己儿子多尔衮的命运呢？她又知不知道乾隆四十三年（1778年）时，乾隆帝正式为多尔衮平反呢？

PRINCIPAL CONCUBINE ABAHAI: IS SHE WILLING TO BE BURIED ALIVE WITH EMPEROR?

In fact, there was another concubine buried in Fuling Imperial Tomb. She was the principal concubine, Abahai. Affections between Nurhaci and Menggu have always been a puzzle. Some people say that Nurhaci was passionately devoted to Menggu while others say that Menggu died from depression due to frustration in love. Through analysis, I think that the latter is more possible to happen. Though Menggu married Nurhaci earlier than another favored concubine, Abahai, it was Abahai instead of Menggu who was upgraded to the principal wife when the second wife of Nurhaci surnamed Fucha died. Moreover, Menggu gave birth to only one child, Hong Taiji, during all her life while Abahai gave birth to three son, i.e. the eldest Ajige, the second Dorgon and the third Dodo. According to these facts, Menggu was not necessarily that most favored concubine. On the contrary, Abahai was the only concubine who Nurhaci wanted to see on his deathbed. The mother's honor increases as her son's position rises. If the son of Abahai, Dorgon, had ascended the throne, the main female figure of Fuling Imperial Tomb would have been another woman.

Abahai, surnamed Wula Nala, was born in the seventeenth year of Emperor Wanli (1589) from a noble family of Wula tribe. Her father, Mantai, was chief of Wula tribe in Haixi. I once lectured in Jilin City and leaders of Wula Street invited me four times to do research there. Abahai's tribe was destroyed six years earlier than Menggu's tribe by Jurchen tirbe of Nurhaci, her husband.

In the twenty-ninth yearof Emperor Wanli (1601) when Abahai was only twelve years old, she married Nurhaci as a concubine, becoming his tenth wife. In the fifth year of Tianming (1620) when Abahai was 19, she was upgraded to the principal concubine and began to support housekeeping. Though her three sons were still young, Nurhaci let each of them manage one whole banner. As foundation of Later Jin, Eight Banner military only had eight banners, of which they just held three. This suggested how deep affection Nurhaci showed to Abahai.

Nurhaci went to Qinghe to bathe in the hot spring for recuperation on July 23 of the eleventh year of Tianming. On August 7, Nurhaci became critically ill. He urgently summoned the principal concubine Abahai to meet him while returning to Shenyang by boat along Taizi River. Nurhaci did see his principal concubine, yet it was too late as he couldn't speak then.

According to historians, after Nurhaci died, Abahai was forced by all princes to be buried together with him, becoming the victim of royal court struggle. During four days before the death of Nurhaci, only the principal concubine Abahai was attending upon him in order. Therefore, she was a fatal opponent for competitive forces of Hong Taiji, Daishan, etc. If they didn't get rid of her, she could make her son ascend the throne with the advantage of Emperor's will, though it may be the desire of Nurhaci. However, Hong Taiji was more mature than the young Dorgon, and better understanding and controlling the political situation. He united other princes to fabricate the will of his father and then became Emperor, and forced Abahai to be buried together with Nurhaci. Manchu then still had the system of burying alive with the dead. Such system was not rare in the feudal society, yet it was applied conditionally, i.e. the wives and concubines to be buried alive with their husband had no children to take care of and were inferior in status. Although Dorgon was young then, he shouldn't know little about all this. Was Abahai willing to be buried alive with Emperor?

If it were as historians analyzed, did Abahai give her last words to her son before she was buried alive? Why did Dorgon and Dodo who controlled massive forces help their brother Hong Taiji? Who planned the burial of their mother in order to gain the reign? Why did they help Fulin, the youngest son of Hong Taiji to secure his throne? It is said the reason why Dorgon did not usurp is that Concubine Zhuang married him, which is now proved to be purely fictitious.

In the seventh year of Emperor Shunzhi (1650), Abahai obtained a posthumous title of "Filial, pious, caring, wise, benevolent and beautiful sage Empress" and her spirit tablet was enshrined in the ancestral temple to accept the sacrifice from her descendents. Unfortunately, such good times didn't last long and in the next year, Dorgon was convicted after death. Emperor Shunzhi once filed the bones of Dorgon to ashes and spread them. However, he didn't dare to restructure Tai Tsu's Mausoleum and risk everyone's condemnation even if he had such desire. As a result, Abahai, whose life was full of twists and turns, has always been with her Khan husband in obscurity, buried in Fuling Imperial Tomb. But did Abahai know what fate her son Dorgon would have? Did she also know that Emperor Qianlong officially rehabilitated for Dorgon in the 3rd year of Qianlong's reign (1778)?

宝顶神树 / 右图
Divine Tree on Blessed Vault / Right

神榆与大清的命运

大约是乾隆时期，在福陵宝顶上栽了一棵榆树，以附会永陵"神榆"。一次偶然的对比，我发现福陵两幅古代地图，有着很大的差别。最明显的就是一幅地图宝顶上有神树，一幅宝顶上没有神树，根据史料推测，这两幅地图形成的时间应该是不同时期的，可能就是以乾隆时期为分界的。福陵昭陵神树都在宝顶上，与福陵、昭陵不同的是，永陵神榆，并不是种在宝顶上，而是种在五个宝顶中间最大的衣冠冢前，两侧四个宝顶呈U形排列，将神榆围在中间。在墓上种树制度，最早可追溯到秦朝，商鞅变法中对墓上种树有明确规定："小夫死以上至大夫，其官爵一等，其墓树，级一树。"小夫的墓上种一棵树，大夫的墓上种八棵树，而没有爵位的人，死后墓上是不能种树的。种树，是给予死者的荣誉。而吴国大夫伍子胥在自刎前说过"必树吾墓上以梓，令可以为器"，可见，在墓上种树古已有之。而清朝，对皇帝棺椁的称呼，还有"梓宫"一词，后来演变成"宝宫"。

因孔子有"思其人，必爱其树"之语，所以墓前种树，在孔子去世以后蔚然成风。而清朝在宝顶上种榆树的原因，不仅是受汉文化影响，还有一个重要的原因，就是榆树与爱新觉罗氏先祖，有一段传奇的渊源。神榆是乾隆皇帝给永陵古榆的封号，永陵是清第一座祖陵，内葬太祖之远祖、高祖、祖父、父等肇兴景显四祖，永陵的主顶上有一棵巨大的榆树。关于这棵榆树，民间有很多传说。传说当年这棵树上附有"悬龙"，恰巧被努尔哈赤的先祖压住，因而才有了后来的大清基业。乾隆皇帝东巡祭祖时，还封它为神树并御书《神树赋》一篇，刻于碑石。盛京将军每月要将神榆的长势和保护情况向皇帝奏

本一次。为附会永陵神树，又在福陵和昭陵宝顶各栽一棵榆树。而神树的命运，也似乎真的与大清的命运息息相关。同治二年（1863年）永陵枝繁叶茂的"神树"被大风吹倒，巨大的树枝将永陵启运殿的屋顶都压坏了。同治皇帝感到此事不吉利，命两位大臣赶往东北，用木墩子撑住神树。然而，所有努力都无济于事，神树最终还是一半生一半枯。而此时的清朝，已经开始衰落。

目前"关外三陵"中长势最好最茂盛的是昭陵神树，而永陵神树，在新中国成立后，被一位解放军的营长砍来生火，那个营长因此受到处分被降为连长，退休后还专门写信说过此事，后悔至极，若不是当年的错误，他可能早成为将军了。而现在福陵神树都是后来又长的，因为福陵宝顶没有塌陷，也因此没有受到什么损坏。值得一提的是，福陵修缮的时候大殿的木结构，柱子外面都包了"树脂"，没有古建筑中的地藏法，没有修旧如旧，这样致使很多建筑后来遭到损坏，尤其是昭陵宝顶修缮时竟然用了水泥，应该用三合土的。我内心感到非常遗憾，古建筑的修缮，不应该是某些人的异想天开。保护古建，古树作为历史见证者，也是不该被忽视的一部分。

清代绘制的福陵全景图／下图
Panoramic View of Fuling Imperial Tomb Drawn in Qing Dynasty / Lower

DIVINE ELM AND FATE OF GREAT QING DYNASTY

During the years of Emperor Qianlong, an elm was planted on Blessed Vault in Fuling Imperial Tomb to follow the example of Yong Mausoleum. By an accidental comparison, I found that the two ancient maps of Fuling Imperial Tomb were quite different. It is quite obvious that there is a tree on Blessed Vault in one map, while there is nothing in the other. According to historical resources, the two maps were created at different times, which might be divided by the reign of Emperor Qianlong. In contrast with Fu and Zhaoling Imperial Tombs, the elm of Yong Mausoleum is planted not on Blessed Vault but in front of the biggest cenotaph. The other four vaults surround the elm in a U-shape. The practice of tree planting can be traced back to Qin Dynasty. And then tree planting on tombs was clearly regulated by Political Reforms of Shang Yang: one tree shall be planted on tomb of Xiaofu (minor official); eight trees shall be planted on tomb of Dafu (senior official); people without titles cannot have trees planted on their tombs. We can see that it is an honor to plant trees on tombs of the deceased. Before committing suicide, Wu Zixu, Dafu of Wu State said, "make sure to plant a catalpa on my tomb and let it grow up." It can be concluded that planting trees on tombs is an ancient tradition. In Qing Dynasty, the coffin of an emperor is called "Catalpa Palace," which later developed into "Blessed Palace."

Confucius had said, "if you miss somebody, you must love his tree." It had formed a tradition to plant trees on tombs after Confucius' death. Planting elms on Burial Bastions is not only influenced by traditional Chinese culture, but also there is another important reason. It is said that there was a legendary story between elms and ancestors of Aisin Gioro. Divine Elm is the title conferred by Emperor Qianlong. Yong mausoleum is the first mausoleum of Qing Dynasty where Tai Tsu's remote ancestor, great-grandfather, grandfather and father of Qianlong were buried. On the summit of Yong Mausoleum, there is a giant elm to which many stories are related. It is said that there was a "suspended dragon" on the elm, which happened to be suppressed by Nurhaci's ancestors. Then there came prosperity of Qing Dynasty. When Emperor Qianlong travelled to the east for ancestral worship, he conferred it as Divine Tree and composed An Ode to Divine Tree, which was inscribed on the stone tablet. Every month, General of Mukden would report the gardening and protection situations of Divine Tree to Emperor. Following the suit of Yong Mausoleum, an elm tree was planted in Fuling Imperial Tomb and Zhaoling Imperial Tomb respectively. It seems that the fate of Divine Tree really had some relationship with that of Qing Dynasty indeed. In the 2nd ruling year of Tongzhi (1863), Divine Tree with luxuriant foliage was blown down by the windstorm, and its huge branches broke the roof of Luck-provoking Hall. Emperor Tongzhi felt uneasy about this event, so he ordered two chancellors to prop up Divine Tree with a block of wood. All their efforts turned out to be in vain, and at last even roots of the Tree were rotten. From that time on, Qing Dynasty began to decline.

Currently, of Three Mausoleums in Shengjing, the most exuberant divine tree is the one in Zhaoling Imperial Tomb. After liberation, the tree of Yong Mausoleum had been chopped by a battalion commander of Liberation Army, who was later descended to company commander. After he retired, he wrote a letter stating it regretfully because if he had not cut it by mistake, he should have been a general long before. Divine Tree in Fuling Imperial Tomb was planted in later time, but was kept very well due to good condition of Blessed Vault. Regret worth mentioning is that wooden structures and columns of the palaces were painted with "resin" during the maintenance of Fuling Imperial Tomb instead of following the principle of repairing as it were by means of earthening, thus a lot of buildings were damaged. To take Blessed Vault of Zhaoling Imperial Tomb for instance, it was repaired with cement instead of triple-combined soil. The renovation of ancient architecture should not be treated randomly. As witnesses of history, these ancient trees and architectures should also be protected as an integral part, which can not be neglected.

大碑楼两侧的古松 / 左页图
Aged Pine Trees beside Great Stele Pavilion / Left Page
2007年4月作者从日本返回后发现古松已死去 / 左下图
Dead Pine in April 2007 after my Visit of Japan / Lower Left
古松的枝干制作成的供游人休息用的座椅 / 右上图
Seats Made out of Branch of Dead Pine / Upper Right
宝城与红墙之间死去的古檀 / 右下图
Dead Ancient Wingceltis between Burial Bastion and Red Wall / Lower Right

站班的古松也是文物

我还专门拍摄过大碑楼两侧的古松，构图时两侧的树显得威严壮观。可惜的是，我去日本做学术研究一年，半年时回国，又去福陵拍摄，发现碑楼东侧的古松已经枯死了，枯死的古松，在天柱山上躺了四年后，被做成了椅子放置在陵寝内供游人休息。而这棵古松当年的风姿，只能留在我的作品里了。

古树，是福陵里的忠诚守护者，他们像忠诚的守陵人一样，世代坚守，寸步不离。这里的古树，见证了中国三百年的历史，它们早已成为陵寝古迹的一部分。据考证，沈阳清福陵当年共栽植的松树约三万余株，占地"九千亩"，与昭陵所栽松树一样，都是油松，而两陵的油松均取自距沈阳百里以外的鞍山——千山的原始森林之中。据记载，当时运往两陵的油松总数达万株，而选树的条件十分苛刻：要求树龄在10年以上，树形高大端庄，侧枝成层，虬曲多姿。所选之树一律树根带土，由专人运送。不仅如此，古松的栽植也十分讲究，根据《大清宝典》中记载，陵区松树有"山树"、"仪树"、"海树"、"荡树"之分。"山树"栽在山周围，"海树"栽植在风水红墙以外，"仪树"是指分列在隆恩门前神道两旁的8棵树，也称"站班树"和"八大朝臣"；"荡树"是指风水红墙里的树，其排列有序，十分整齐。此外，对栽种后松树的管理也十分严格，对树木逐一建立档案记载，凡枯死、倒伏、砍伐者一律上报盛京将军批准后才能处理。不准多种，也不准少种，遵循死一棵补种一棵的原则。但是，清朝灭亡以后，又历经战乱，福陵古松以前有3万余棵，到现在只剩1600多棵了，每一棵都有编号。历史上盗伐陵树的案件很多，而现在随着人们保护环境意识的增强，古松得到了应有的保护与重视。站在方城上，依然可见红墙外那些威仪的忠诚陵寝卫士。

然而，现在的很多人并不了解古代帝王陵寝的种树制度，曾经在陵区里种植了大量的新树，使陵区的古松显得杂乱而失去了以往的威严阵势。我们应该尊重历史原貌，保护古松，既是保护环境，又是保护古迹，保护那一段尘封的历史。

方城东侧的古树／左页图
Aged Trees in the East Side of Square City / Left Page
20 世纪 30 年代与 90 年代神桥两侧的古松的比较／下图
Aged Pines along Spirit Bridge in 1930's in contrast with the Ones in 1990's / Lower

GUARDIAN PINES ARE ALSO ANTIQUITY

I specifically took pictures for old pines on both sides of Great Stele Pavilion, in framing of which thses trees looked dignified and magnificent. Unfortunately, I went to Fuling Imperial Tomb for shooting after six months of academic study in Japan, and the old pine to the east of the Pavilion turned out to have been dead. Although the dead pine was made into benches for tourists inside the mausoleum after four years of lying down on Mount Tianzhu. the grace of that old pine could only stay in my work.

The aged trees are loyal guardians in Fuling Imperial Tomb, and they secure this place firmly, never giving up like most devoted mausoleum keepers. They have witnessed three hundred years of Chinese history and already become a part of mausoleum monument. According to research, there were totally thirty thousand pines in Fuling Imperial Tomb covering "nine thousand acres;" they were all Chinese pines like the ones in Zhaoling Imperial Tomb; the pipes in these two mausoleums were all from the primeval forest of Anshan — Mount Qian, hundreds of miles away from Shenyang. It is recorded that the total number of pines transported to these two mausoleums was more than ten thousand and the requirements of choosing pines are very harsh: 10 years old, of tall and stately shape, with multi-layer side branches and coiled postures. All the selected trees are delivered with soil by special working force. Moreover, the plantation of these pines was also very particular, and according to Collection of Great Qing, the pines in the Mausoleum could be divided into "hill tree," "posture tree," "sea tree," and "swing tree." Hill trees are planted around the hill; sea trees outside the omen red walls; posture trees refer to the 8 pines on both sides of Spirit Path in front of Eminent Favor Gate, also known as "standing trees" and "Eight courtiers," and swing trees refer to the trees in neat sequence inside the omen red walls. In addition, management of planted pine trees is also very strict: files for every pine will be created, and all the dead, lodging, chopped down trees must be submitted to General of Shengjing for approval. The principle is strictly followed that no more or no less trees can be planted and only one pine can be planted when one died. However, there are only 1600 aged pines left now, and no longer thirty thousand pines in the past, due to influencecs of the end of Qing Dynasty and the later wars, and each tree has a number. In the past, there were many cases of illegal logging of mausoleum trees, but now with the increasing awareness of environmental protection, these old pines are well protected. Viewing over Square City, you can still see these loyal and solemn mausoleum guards standing outside the red walls.

However, many people nowadays do not understand the planting system of ancient imperial mausoleums and plant a large number of new trees there, so that the aged pine trees in the Mausoleum are messy without their previous dignity. We should respect the original appearance of history and protect these old pines, which is not only to protect our environment, but also to preserve ancient ruins and a passage of unsealed history.

雪罩龙潭／上图
Snow-covered Dragon Lake / Upper
一百单八蹬两侧的古松／右页图
Aged Pine Trees beside the 108 Steps / Right Page

卧虎藏龙

陵中有卧虎，暗湖似藏龙。关于福陵的种种玄机，有很多都是随着岁月的冲刷而渐渐显影成像的，仿佛是拍摄中一次长久的曝光，终于在流年的尘埃中被我发现，在我心上留下了惊艳的一瞥。

福陵后，有一个龙尾湖，龙尾湖是在山间沟壑中，人为修筑堤坝而成的水面，过去这里叫龙尾沟。我小时候以为福陵只有山没有水，后来随着对陵寝学的逐渐研究，我知道，帝王陵寝，一般都是依山傍水，更有"有山无水休寻地"的说法，而在古地图上，我也见到福陵周围是有水的，因此我一直在寻找福陵的水。一次在隆恩门上拍摄的时候，我发现了福陵前的龙滩，后来我见到了龙尾湖，偶然又想到福陵里那只卧着的可爱的老虎石象生，可以说，福陵里真是卧虎藏龙。

我再次感叹于福陵的神秘，如今的龙尾湖成了景区，而龙潭前依然有很多人垂钓，尤其是晚上，那些点灯垂钓的人构成了这里的风景之一。往日百官下马地，而今日我的镜头里却是车水马龙，热闹繁华，历史如梦，果真如此。

Dragon Lake in Sunset / Left

CROUCHING TIGERS AND HIDDEN DRAGONS

It seems that there are tigers crouching in the Mausoleum and dragons hiding in the lake. With time passing by, many of the mysteries of Fuling Imperial Tomb finally fade out themselves in the condensed dust of history, leaving a stunning glance in my heart, which resembles a long exposure of a picture shooting.

There is a Dragon Tail Lake behind Fuling Imperial Tomb, an expanse of water in the valley behind an artificial dam, which was once called Dragon Tail Valley. I thought in my childhood that there was only mountain without water around Fuling Imperial Tomb. With my further research into mausoleums, I began to know that mausoleums would surely reside in a place with mountains and waters. There is even a saying that goes like this, "never find resting site in a mountain without water." And there was water around Fuling Imperial Tomb on ancient maps. So I have been looking for water of Fuling Imperial Tomb all the time. I noticed Dragon Beach in front of Fuling Imperial Tomb when I took photos at Eminent Favor Hall. Later on, I saw Dragon Tail Lake, and accidentally I associated it with these crouching tigers statues in Fuling Imperial Tomb, which coincides with the geomantic situation of Crouching Tigers and Hidden Dragons.

Once again, I marveled at the mysteries of Fuling Imperial Tomb. And now Dragon Tail Lake serves as a scenic spot, where many people still come for fishing. When dark casts over the Lake, the fishing lights scattered here and there, composing a beautiful scenery. A place where all officials once had to dismount now becomes a populated place in my camera, which well demonstrates the dramatic changing history.

紫气东来 / 左页图
Purple Air Coming from the East (a Propitious Omen) / Left Page

天赐的紫气东来

关于封面的这幅紫气东来，我心里也有很多感慨。好的摄影作品，很大程度上应该说是"上天赐予的"。一件成功的摄影作品背后，重叠着各样的努力和机遇，缺一则不可。

就好比在拥有了精湛的摄影技术这一条件下，如果没有一架各项机能优良的相机，技术也只能是困于樊笼中的飞鸟，并无用武之地。

有了成熟的技术，同时具备一台优质的相机，却还是远远不够的，因为两者都是客观而又相对的，是可以随着时代的发展而不断更新提高的，这时还需要摄影者本身的主观力量——信念、胆量和体力。很多作品的拍摄过程都不是一帆风顺的，而是充满了惊险与波折，路况堪舆、气候恶劣的时候，摄影者还需要足够的力量去支撑自己定格一瞬间的永恒。

当有了好的技术、好的相机，也有足够的胆量和体力时，没有一定的社会地位也不能够拍出优秀的作品，门票的昂贵让很多爱好者望而却步，某些禁止拍摄的神秘文物更是让人在摄影之时倍感无奈。如果当所有这些条件都具备了，偏偏此时没有恰到好处的天气也还是不行，正所谓"万事俱备只欠东风"。于某一个时间点上，错落的光线和大自然的色彩达到了完美的统一之时，才能够拍摄出有生命质感的精彩影像，那是一种多么难得的与天地万物的缘分啊，可以说，好的作品是天赐的。

我常常对别人说，一个成功的摄影家是一个全才，需要有泰山挑夫的体力，于奔波跋涉中保持旺盛的精力；要有猎人的眼睛，敏锐地洞悉摄影时的角度与背景；要有奥运射击冠军的精准，于千钧一发之际捕获最难得的瞬间；要有哲学家的头脑，巧妙地让图片背后深藏的故事浮凸显影；要有文物学家的鉴赏力，于众多影像中挑选最合宜、最精彩的一个。

入摄影之门三十余年，在这个完整的摄影流程中，我无数次按下快门，快意于浮生之作；无数次了然领悟，惊觉所学之无穷。透过镜头我读懂了流年，存志于更远。摄影如同人生之路，也有跌宕起伏，从胶片转向数码，已然淘汰一批人，我很庆幸，自己仍在其列，但是更多时候，我觉得自己在这条路上，还只是个小学生。

BLESSED PURPLE AIR COMING FROM THE EAST

The photo of Purple Air Coming from the East on the book cover provokes running tides inside my heart. A masterpiece of a photograph, to some extent, is "a gift from God." In order to shoot a successful photograph, efforts of various kinds and transient opportunities ought to depend on and complement each other, like a master craftsman who cannot be in short of excellent tools. How can a master photographer take splendid photos with a camera with poor performance? Techniques create nothing wonderful without good tools.

Acquainted with mastery techniques and a high-quality camera, one is still far away from taking good photos, because they are comparatively objective, which are developing and improving constantly. What's more, the subjective strength of the photographer, his faith, courage and physical strength matter much. Many successful shootings are not smooth and certain in its due course; they are full of ups and downs, such as rugged roads, bad-tempered weathers. And the photographer must also have enough power to support himself and freeze the moments in the frame of eternity.

In addition to good techniques, high-quality cameras and also courage and strength, certain social status is necessary for a photographer to achieve the aims to shoot good photos. Expensive tickets block many fans, and the rarely exhibited relics which are banned from photographing leave even more regrets for a photographer.

If and when all these conditions are met with, favorable weather is important to decide your success, as the saying goes, "All that is needed is an east wind." At certain time, when scattered lights and colors of nature can match perfectly, one can create images full of vivid life, a masterpiece of nature and techniques. Therefore, a masterpiece is "a gift from God."

I often tell people, a successful photographer must be an all-rounder, who is in good possession of energetic physical power of a porter of Mount Tai enduring hardship, keen eyes of a hunter without missing any ideal angles and perspectives, accuracy of an Olympic shooting champion capturing the most precious moments, mind of a philosopher cleverly highlighting the hidden stories behind pictures, and competence of an art collector to appreiciate and identify the most appropriate and most brilliant among a number of images.

I have been engaged in photography for more than thirty years. In this continuous process of photographing, for numercus times I press down the shutter and indulge myself in the marvelous creations of nature, and for numerous times I suddenly come home to the idea that there are far more out there for me to learn. Through camera, I understand what running time is and I know how to goal higher and further. Photography is like the road of life, full of ups and downs. From analog to digital, many people lag far behind, but fortunately I still keep pace with the advancing technology. However, for most of time, I know I'm still a pupil who needs to learn more.

结语
——四十五年分之一秒

这些年，我对福陵，在内心有着更深厚的情感寄托。从儿时的记忆，到后来的写生与拍摄，占据了我生命中的一部分时间。依然记得，年少的我坐车一辆公车，背着画夹，穿越半个城市，来到红门紧闭的福陵外写生的感觉；依然记得，我扛着相机，设备沉重而脚步轻快的莫大喜悦；更不能忘记，捧着我拍摄出来的福陵申遗的照片的内心激动。这些细微之处，都是我生命之中的往事。

四十五年，说长也长，说短也短，对于人生，它却似乎过于短暂而匆忙。我从意气风发的少年，到壮志凌云的青年，转眼，已进入沉稳干练的不惑之年。人生，仿若一盏新茶，开始的时候，虚浮飘摇，逐渐沉淀，而后落定。这个过程，有苦涩，有香甜，品的人不同，所得之味也不同。待到茶凉，回味起来又各有差别。那些散落在时光里的年华，再也无从追寻，曾一度彷徨，生命的没有痕迹，就像天空有鸟飞过，怎么证明呢？生的虚无，而死又永恒，我试图抓住些什么，但是我能抓住什么呢？

这些年，经历多了，让我对人生的感悟也多了，参加的葬礼多了，对生死的理解也多了。虽早将生死看开，看透，甚至可以说是置之度外，工作起来有点不要命的感觉。内心却时常焦急，人生之路，日已偏西，我还在途中艰难跋涉。过了如日中天的盛年，谁不渴望在日落西山时会有满天晚霞，渴望给这生命留下些印记？有生之年，我庆幸，我找到了属于自己的方式，去记忆那些零碎的光景，拼起时光的片段。无论是画画还是摄影，它们都使早已消失的时间，在某一刻，变成了实实在在，可以触摸的真实，这些都是我生命的痕迹，我的生命。越来越多地按动快门，

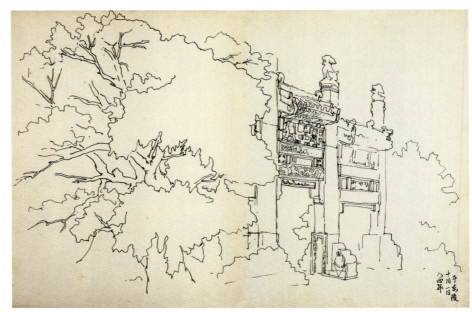

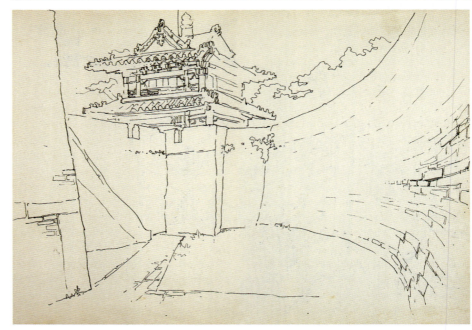

17岁画福陵牌坊（1984年）／上图
Paifang of Fuling Imperial Tomb Drawn at the Age of 17（1984）／ Upper
17岁画福陵月牙城（1984年）／下图
Crescent City of Fuling Imperial Tomb Drawn at the Age of 17（1984）／ Lower

那"咔嚓"、"咔嚓"的声音，对于我是那么的悦耳，因为我知道，在这微小的一声一声中，我抓住了一秒又一秒的时间。

在福陵与昭陵中拍照，早已成为我的一种消遣，我翻阅多年来积存下来的照片，重新审视我熟悉的福陵与昭陵，竟然发现，它们对于我如同新交的挚友，有熟悉的记忆，却有新的内容，仿佛等待我继续用生命对它们进行探索与发现。每一张照片，都是我曾经小心翼翼逮住的时间，我生命的四十五年分之一秒。有时候，我会为这短短的一秒钟而欣喜若狂。当年我在鲁美当助教的时候工资只有四百块钱，每次拍摄用的胶卷却都要上千元，回想这么多年来拍摄的照片，最后用上的竟多数是近十年拍摄的，而过去那二十年似乎是浪费了。仔细一想，也不尽然，一个神枪手，若不是之前浪费了很多子弹，最终也不会成为神枪手。这样想，我又释然了。

四十五年，置于整个历史洪流之中，不过是白驹过隙，须臾即逝，于我却是整个生命。我为四川"5·12"大地震贡献了一枚纪念章，也贡献出了我的健康，严重的腿伤导致我至今都不能再登高，时常忍受着神经压迫的尖锐痛苦，而我能为我最亲最近的家乡贡献些什么呢？我将我生命的某一瞬，定格在那一张张充满鲜活记忆的照片中，留给后人的或许只是史料，留给自己的却是一种使命，我必须完成。纵使在福陵拍摄已经有二十余年了，但是我仍然没有拍全传说中的"福陵八景"，只是这些年的工作，不是我一个人努力的结果，没有沈阳市城市建设管理局对我的全力支持，没有福陵全体工作人员的配合，我也不可能完成这一秒一秒的工作，即使有了这一秒时间，如果没有适合的天气和光线，我同样不能完成这一秒的工作，可以说这一秒是"天时地利人和"同时具备才能完成的。为此，我内心充满了感激。

学地质的人，愿意用一小时来形容地球的存在，那么人类的存在仅相当于两秒钟。而我的存在，至于整个人类就更微乎其微了。但是，建筑是永恒的。我用我生命的四十五年分之一秒，记录了福陵与昭陵的永恒，每一秒，都是古人智慧的闪光。纵使生命终归是一捧流沙，人类还是将自己的微渺汇集成了这些建筑的伟大，供后人尊崇与膜拜。而我则为使这伟大得到永恒的延续而努力，而乐此不疲，疲而不倦。

斗转星移，昔日英雄横刀立马的时代早已一去不复返。天生英武的努尔哈赤一手造就的大清王朝经历了康乾盛世的无比繁华，也见证了丧权辱国的痛苦历史。如今，千秋功过已成过眼烟云，只有巍然而立的福陵仍在以其独特的方式向世人呈现着独具特色的文化，让人幻想曾经弓腰驼背辛苦劳作的匠人，幻想皇子皇孙率领群臣浩浩荡荡在此拜谒的威仪，幻想守陵人世代护陵的那份寂寞与忠诚。

中国古人基于人死而灵魂不灭的观念，无论任何阶层对陵寝皆精心构筑。早已使陵寝建筑与绘画、书法、雕刻等诸艺术门派融为一体，成为反映多种艺术成就的综合体。我热爱建筑，研究建筑，而对于近水楼台的家乡福陵，也多着一分偏爱。在清朝统治的二百多年间，福陵作为皇室从事礼制活动的主要场所，无论是建筑遗存，还是其所包含的历史史实，都是研究清朝陵寝制度、陵寝礼仪乃至清初的殉葬制度、祭祀制度、职官体制以及政治、经济、文化等方面的实物资料，记录着明末、清朝及民国年间的历史。在我心里，清福陵不仅仅是中国帝陵建筑的重要组成部分，也是中国历史文化的最好见证。

福陵的建筑结构之严谨，雕刻之精细，无处不凝聚着我国古代劳动人民的智慧和技艺，无处不体现了我国古代建筑艺术的优秀传统和独特风格，无处不反映着中华民族的高度智慧和创造才能。漫步在陵区里，我内心时刻充满了自豪，这是一种家族的自豪感，是刻在骨子里的荣光。我在内心，把它当成私有财产一样珍爱。在漫长的历史进程中，陵区受到保护，却也有一定程度的损坏，这是随着历史厚度的增加而无法避免的。由于不能掌握当时的技艺，后世的修缮，也不可能尽善尽美，使我常常生出遗憾。希望此生，以我微薄的努力，使更多的人对这些建筑与文化能有更深刻的了解，也可以使家乡的这些文化遗产，得到更加长久妥善的保护。如此，我所有的辛苦努力，就都值得了……

到此书出版的时候，我对书中的图片、文字、版式等都不是很满意，研究福陵的工作不是我人生的全部，实在缺少时间，只能仓促交稿，定有缺憾，留后世评说吧！

公元二〇一一年春
于九平书屋

EPILOGUE
— ONE SECOND OUT OF 45 YEARS

For these years, I have a deep affection for Fuling Imperial Tomb. From the memory of childhood to the later painting and photography, it takes a great part of my life. I still remember how I felt when I took the paper sketchpad folders, crossed half a city on bus to Fuling Imperial Tomb, whose red door was tightly closed; I still remember the delight when I carried my heavy camera and other devices with light footsteps; I still remember how excited I became when photos of Fuling Imperial Tomb were used for applying for World Heritage. These details are all deeply rooted in my mind throughout my life.

45 years is both long and short. It is transient and hasty for a whole life. In an instant, I'm stepping into my mature and experienced forties now from a high-spirited and vigorous juvenile and then an ambitious youth. Life is like a cup of hot tea. At the beginning, these delicate leaves are floating and swaying. Gradually, they began to sediment and then settle down. From the process, different people will have different tastes: some people think it bitter and others think it sweet. When the tea cools, aftertaste is different again. You can never call back those years which are already lost in the past. I have been hesitating as there is no trace of life left, just like a bird darting through the sky. Life is nihilism and death is eternity. I try to catch something, but what can I catch?

For these years, I experienced a lot and I understood much in life. The more funerals I attended, the more I understood about life and death. Despite these retrospective deliberations, I still work desperately and feel anxious in mind from time to time. The sun has set in the west and I still waded on the way. After passing by the heyday of my life, I really want to have a splendid sunset in my later life. I am fortunate as I find my own method to recollect those memories and those segments of my life. Paintings or photos fix time and turn it into tangible reality, which are all the traces of my life. The pleasing sound of the shutter clicks grasp one second after another and then I know I'm not wasting my life.

Taking photos of Fuling Imaperial Tomb and Zhaoling Imperial Tomb has become a pastime for me. I like to browse the photos accumulated for years to review these familiar and pleasant memory, among which there is something not only new but also familiar to me, like newly-made friends, who are there waiting and expecting me to explore and discover them. Each photo is a second I carefully captured in my last 45 years. Sometimes, I craze over a short second I seized. When I was an assistant instructor at Luxun Fine Arts Institute, my salary then was only 400 yuan. But every time the films I used for shooting would cost more than thousand yuan. Thinking back, I only compiled in this book the photos I took in these recent ten years, and the

17岁画福陵西侧石牌坊（1984年）
Stone Paifang to the West of Fuling Imperial Tomb Drawn at the Age of 17 (1984)

photos of those past two decades seem to be a waste. Thinking it twice, however, it was unnecessarily the case. A sharpshooter must waste a lot of bullets before he becomes an expert. Then I feel better and rest at ease.

45 years is comparatively a short time in history, but for me it's my whole life. I contributed a memorial souvenir badge to the 5.12 Earthquake happened in Sichuan. Also, I contributed my health because my knee suffered from comminuted fracture. Even today, I cannot climb high and often bear sharp pains coming from the pressed nerves. But what can I do for my hometown? I will frame some seconds of my life into photos with fresh and vivid memories. What I have left to our later generation is probably only some historical data, while for me it is a mission which I must fulfill. Even though I have been shooting pictures of Fuling Imperial Tomb for more than twenty years, I am still not able to shoot all the legendary "Fuling Imperial Tomb Eight Scenes." However, all the works of these years were not completed all by myself: I could not finish all these works without full support of Shenyang Urban Construction Authority and cooperation of all the staff in Fuling Imperial Tomb; I still could not do this one-second job if the weather and light are not appropriate even if I have time. It can be said that this one-second requires "good timing, geographical convenience and good human relations." Accordingly, I am much filled with gratitude.

Those who specialize in geology would like to describe existence of the Earth with "one hour." In that case, existence of human beings is about two seconds. Hence, my existence, or existence of our human beings is even tiny. But architecture will last. I record eternity of Fuling Imperial Tomb and Zhaoling Imperial Tomb with one second out of my 45 years. From each second, you can see the shining wisdom of ancient people. Life is like shifting sand and human beings collect these tiny moments and build them into magnificent buildings for their later generations to worship and admire. To make such greatness continue for ever, I work hard at it, enjoy it and never feel tired.

With time flying, the past heroic times has gone forever. Great Qing Dynasty, founded by Nurhaci, had experienced its unparalleled prosperity of Kangxi and Qianlong, and had

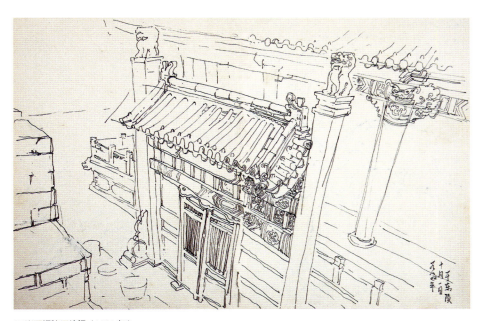

17岁画福陵二柱门（1984年）
Dual Pillar Gate of Fuling Imperial Tomb Drawn at the Age of 17 (1984)

also witnessed its humiliating and sovereignty forfeiting history. Now, all merits find no trace as fleeting cloud; only the imposing Fuling Imperial Tomb still present its unique culture with its own style, from which we can fantasize the craftsmen working arduously on the sites and the imperial descendents holding grand ceremony to worship their ancestors and the loneliness and fidelity of the Mausoleum guards.

According to the idea held by ancient Chinese that one's spirit will still exist after one dies, people of any class in the past all paid great attention to their careful building of tombs. Tomb construction, painting, calligraphy and sculpture form an integration which can reflect artistic achievement

福陵在辽宁省沈阳市的位置／上图
Location of Fuling Imperial Tomb of Qing Dynasty in Shenyang, Liaoning Province / Upper
辽宁省沈阳市在中国的位置／左图
Location of Shenyang, Liaoning Province in China / Left

of our ancestor. I love architecture and thus study it. Fuling Imperial Tomb is in my hometown and I attach greater affection to it. During over 200 years under the Reign of Qing Dynasty, Fuling Imperial Tomb remained as the main site of imperial ceremonies, and the architectural heritages and historical facts there are physical sources for study of mausoleum system, funeral rites, institution of burying the alive with the dead, fete system, ranking system, as well as politics and economics, and they have documented histories of late Ming Dynasty, Qing Dynasty and Republic of China. In my heart, Fuling Imperial Tomb is not only a key part of imperial mausoleum architecture, but also the best witness of Chinese history and culture.

Strict architectural structure and delicacy of carvings of Fuling Imperial Tomb all shine with wisdoms and skills of ancient Chinese workers as well as excellent architectural traditions and unique styles of ancient Chinese architectural art. Strolling around in Mausoleum, I am full of pride, which is a kind of family glory engraved in my bone. In my heart, I deem it my private possession. But in the long historical process, Mausoleum area is damaged to a certain degree even though it is under protection, which is unavoidable. It's a pity that since we could not grasp skills of these ancient architectures, our later maintenance could not make it as complete as before. I hope I can contribute my effort to promoting people's understanding about architecture, so that these cultural heritages can be protected properly in long run. In this way, all my painstaking efforts are paid off …

Till publication of this book, I am still not much satisfied with these pictures, texts and layout. The research on Fuling Imperial Tomb is not my whole life, and I can do nothing but deliver these pictures and writings in haste, due to lack of time. The book will for sure have its regrettable shortcomings, however, criticism from readers are all welcome.

At Jiuping Study
in the Spring of 2009

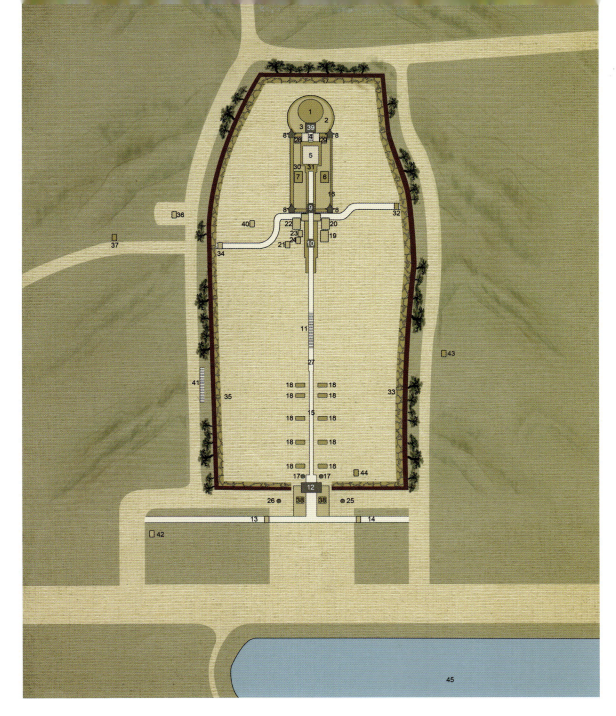

福陵平面图
Ichnography of Fuling Imperial Tomb

1. 宝顶　　　　　　Blessed Vault
2. 宝城　　　　　　Blessed Bastion
3. 月牙城　　　　　Crescent City
4. 大明楼　　　　　Grand Ming Tower
5. 隆恩殿　　　　　Eminent Favor Hall
6. 东配殿　　　　　East Side-hall
7. 西配殿　　　　　West Side-hall
8. 角楼　　　　　　Turrets
9. 隆恩门　　　　　Eminent Favor Gate
10. 神功圣德碑楼　　Stele Pavilion of Divine Merits
11. 一百单八蹬　　　108 Steps
12. 正红门　　　　　Front Red Gate
13. 西石牌坊　　　　West Stone Paifang
14. 东石牌坊　　　　East Stone Paifang
15. 神道　　　　　　Spirit Path
16. 方城马道　　　　Horse Track of Square City
17. 华表　　　　　　Huabiaos
18. 石象生　　　　　Stone Animal Statues
19. 膳房　　　　　　Food House
20. 茶房　　　　　　Tea House
21. 涤器房　　　　　Ware-washing House
22. 果房　　　　　　Fruit House
23. 齐班房　　　　　Qi Ban Fang (Tomb Guards House)
24. 饽饽房　　　　　Bo Bo Fang (Pastry House)
25. 外东华表　　　　Outside East-side Huabiao
26. 外西华表　　　　Outside West-side Huabiao
27. 神桥　　　　　　Spirit Bridge
28. 二柱门　　　　　Dual Pillar Gate
29. 石五供　　　　　Stone Five Offerings
30. 焚帛亭　　　　　Silk Burning Pavilion
31. 隆恩殿前石狮　　Stone Lions in Front of Eminent Favor Hall
32. 东红门　　　　　East Red Gate
33. 东围墙　　　　　East Enclosure Wall
34. 西红门　　　　　West Red Gate
35. 西围墙　　　　　West Enclosure Wall
36. 石龟　　　　　　Stone Turtle
37. 西下马碑　　　　West Dismounting Tablet
38. 石狮　　　　　　Stone Lions
39. 地宫影壁　　　　Screen Wall of Underground Palace
40. 石桩　　　　　　Stone Stake
41. 外一百单八蹬　　Outside 108 Steps
42、43. 三字体下马碑　Dismounting Tablets with Inscriptions of Three Languages
44. 五字体下马碑　　Dismounting Tablets with Inscriptions of Five Languages
45. 龙潭　　　　　　Longtan (Dragon Lake)

注解

注解 1：语出《论语·雍也》，"知者乐水，仁者乐山；知者动，仁者静；知者乐，仁者寿"。知，同智。知者，达于事理而周流无滞，有似于水，故乐水。仁者，安于义理而厚重不迁，有似于山，故乐山。也有将"五行"之说引入者，云："知者属土，故乐水；仁者属木，故乐山。"关于三个乐字的读音，也一直存在争议。可以明确的是前两个乐字音相同，有说音 yao，也有说音 yue 的，属于通假字，第三乐字则取本意，音也为现代的 le。

注解 2：黄帝陵：是中华民族始祖黄帝轩辕氏的陵寝，相传黄帝得道升天，故此陵寝为衣冠冢。位于陕西黄陵县城北桥山；1961 年，国务院公布为全国第一批全国重点文物保护单位，编为"古墓葬第一号"，号称"天下第一陵"。我在 2005 年，规划延安的时候去的黄帝陵。

炎帝陵：炎帝陵一共有三个，分别是"湖南省炎陵县炎帝陵"、"陕西省宝鸡市炎帝陵"和"山西省高平市炎帝陵"。我是在 2005 年，为研究中国广告史去的宝鸡炎帝陵。

大禹陵：大禹陵位于绍兴稽山门外，距城 3 公里。大禹陵本身是一座规模宏大的古典风格建筑群，由禹陵、禹祠、禹庙三部分组成，占地 40 余亩，建筑面积两千六百多平方米，被列为中国文物保护单位。我也是 2005 年，研究中国广告史的时候去的大禹陵。

少昊陵：为了研究中国广告史，我到过不少陵寝。少昊陵，也是那时候去的。少昊，黄帝之子，建都穷桑，后徙曲阜，在位 84 年，寿百岁而终，葬于鲁故城东门之外的寿丘，位于曲阜城东 4 公里的旧县村东北，陵阔 28.5 米，高 8.73 米，顶立 12 米，形如金字塔，有"中国金字塔"之称。

秦始皇陵：我是在 1991 年研究中国广告史的时候，去的秦始皇陵，秦始皇陵位于距西安市 30 多千米的临潼县城以东的骊山脚下。史书记载：秦始皇赵政从 13 岁即位时就开始营建陵园，由丞相李斯主持规划设计，大将章邯监工，修筑时间长达 38 年，工程之浩大、气魄之宏伟，创历代封建统治者奢侈厚葬之先例。

汉武帝陵：汉武帝刘彻是历史上可以和秦始皇相提并论的很有才略的封建帝王，他的陵寝茂陵位于西安市西北 40 公里的兴平市（原兴平县）城东北南位乡茂陵村。公元前 139 年至前 87 年间建成，历时 53 年，现为全国重点文物保护单位。我在 1996 年的时候和 2005 年 10 月研究中国广告史时去两次到过汉武帝陵。

光武帝陵：东汉光武帝刘秀（前 6—后 57）字文叔，南阳蔡阳（今湖北枣阳西南人）高祖九世孙。光武帝陵，当地人称刘秀坟，在河南孟津县铁谢村附近。南依邙山，北濒黄河。陵寝为高大的土冢，周围 1400 米，高 20 米，古柏千余株，苍劲挺拔，阴郁幽静。我是 2004 年，在河南荥阳市讲学的时候去的。

唐太宗陵：唐太宗李世民是唐朝第二代皇帝，他的陵寝与清朝开国皇帝皇太极的陵寝有着相同的名字，同为昭陵，唐昭陵是陕西关中"唐十八陵"中规模最大的一座，位于陕西省礼泉县城东北 22.5 公里的九嵕山上。1991 年，毕业考察，我专门去的唐昭陵。

唐高宗与武则天陵：武则天是中国历史上唯一的女皇帝，同时也是继位年龄最大（67 岁即位），寿命最长的皇帝之一（终年 82 岁）。唐高宗时为皇后、唐中宗和唐睿宗时为皇太后，后自立为武周皇帝，改"唐"为"周"，定都洛阳，史称"武周"或"南周"，705 年退位，死后要求与唐高宗李治合葬。陵寝位于西安乾县。乾陵，是中国乃至世界上独一无二的一座两朝帝王、一对夫妻皇帝合葬陵。建于公元 684 年，历时 23 年才修建完成。1991 年，毕业考察的时候，我专门考察了唐代的陵寝建筑，对乾陵的无字丰碑感叹至今。

宋太祖赵匡胤陵：赵匡胤（927—976），涿州（今河北省涿县）人。他曾是后周王朝的殿前都点检，领宋州归德军节度使，执掌兵权。公元 960 年，他发动"陈桥兵变"，即帝位，称国号"宋"，建立了宋王朝，定都河南开封。宋太祖死于公元 976 年，葬于巩义市宋陵陵区，陵名永昌。我也是 2005 年，在河南巩义市讲学的时候，顺便考察了永昌陵。

宋神宗赵顼陵：赵顼自幼"好学请问，至日晏忘食"。当太子时就喜读《韩非子》，1067—1085 年在位。死后葬于永裕陵，1085 年建造，该陵石刻是宋陵晚期造像的代表，陵中石狮的造型和雕工，在宋陵诸石刻中，位列榜首。人们品评宋陵石雕说："东陵狮子，西陵象，滹沱河上好石羊"。我同样 2005 年，在河南荥阳市讲学的时候，专门到永裕陵，为的是一看那里的石刻。

宋哲宗赵煦陵：宋哲宗赵煦（1076—1100），北宋第七位皇帝，宋神宗第六子，原名佣，曾被封为延安郡王。永泰陵位于巩县芝田乡八陵村村南，东北距芝田镇八华里，东南距永裕陵约 400 米。永泰陵遭到金朝的多次破坏，最残忍的一次，宋哲宗的尸骨也被露掷在永泰陵外，后为臣子包裹重新放置陵中，今日的永泰陵也只剩下一个光秃秃的土丘了。这是我在河南荥阳市讲学时和其他宋朝陵寝一起考察的。

成吉思汗陵：成吉思汗陵在内蒙古鄂尔多斯市伊金霍洛旗甘德利草原上，距东胜区 70 公里。蒙古族盛行"密葬"，所以真正的成吉思汗陵究竟在何处始终是个谜。现今的成吉思汗陵是一座衣冠冢，它经过多次迁移，直到 1954 年才由湟中县的塔尔寺迁回故地伊金霍洛旗，北距包头市 185 公里。1997 年，我在内蒙古奈曼旗讲学的时候特意去拜谒的，距今已有 4 年多了。

明孝陵：明孝陵在南京市东郊紫金山（钟山）南麓独龙阜玩珠峰下，茅山西侧。明朝开国皇帝朱元璋和皇后马氏合葬于此。明孝陵是现存建筑规模最大的古代帝王陵寝之一，其陵寝制度既继承了唐宋及之前帝陵"依山为陵"的制度，又通过改方坟为圜丘，开创了陵寝建筑"前方后圆"的基本格局。那是 1996 年，我在南京熊猫电子讲课的时候，顺便去考察的。

明十三陵：明朝皇帝的墓葬群，因葬有十三位皇帝而得名。在北京西北郊昌平区境内的燕山山麓的天寿山。自永乐七年（1409）五月始做长陵，到明朝最后一帝崇祯葬入思陵止，230 多年间，先后修建了十三座皇帝寝、七座妃子墓、一座太监墓。共埋葬了十三位皇帝、二十三位皇后、二位太子、三十余名妃嫔、一位太监。明十三陵，是我在 1998 年陪父母郊游的时候专程去看的。

注解 3：龙脉：努尔哈赤及其子孙认为，后金乃至大清王朝的帝业渊源于长白山，长白山脉蜿蜒向西南，派生出赫图阿拉老城所在的桥山、沈阳所在的辉山，这是建立帝王基业的"龙脉"，也称之为"龙岗"。

注解 4：《太宗实录》：顺治六年（1649 年）正月初八日，清廷命纂修《太宗实录》，以大学士范文程、刚林、祁充格、洪承畴、冯铨、宁完我、宋权为总裁官，学士王铎、查布海等人为副总裁官。

注解 5：《清实录》：《清实录》，全称《大清历朝实录》，4484卷，《清实录》系清代历朝的官修编年体史料汇编。主要是选录各时期上谕和奏疏，皇帝的起居、婚丧、祭祀、巡幸等活动亦多载入，已编成的十二朝实录，篇幅不等，若十种之间相差颇为悬殊。各朝实录记事细目多寡不均，但主要类别大多相同，举凡政治、经济、文化、军事、外交及自然现象等众多方面的内容皆有。

注解6：《黑图档》：清代盛京总管内务府的档案，为盛京总管内务府同北京总管内务府、盛京将军、奉天府府尹、盛京五部等衙门来往公文的抄存稿簿，反映了盛京总管内务府承办皇室、宫廷事务的详细活动，是研究清代东北地方政治和经济状况、盛京在清代历史上的特殊地位、皇室经济形态等的珍贵史料。

注解7：棂星，原作灵星，灵星即天田星，为祈求丰年，汉高祖规定祭天先祭灵星。宋代则以祭天的礼仪来尊重孔子，后来又改灵星为棂星。何谓棂星门？原来棂星即古代天文学上之"文星"，以此命名，表示天下文人学士集学于此。夫子庙的棂星门与曲阜孔庙的棂星门一样，是庙的第一道大门。

注解8：牌楼的"楼"：是指飞檐起脊的部分，有一、三、五、七、九、十一楼之分。有一间的牌楼，有三间的牌楼，一定是单数而不用双数。一般封建皇帝都建到九楼。

注解9：《封氏闻见记》，全书共十卷。唐代"封演"撰。此书史料价值颇高，编排极有条理，凡一百门，皆两字为题，如道教、儒教、文字、贡举等等。所涉及范围很广，既有科举、铨选等政治制度，又有壁记、烧尾等官场习俗，也有婚仪、服饰、饮食、打球、拔河、绳技等社会生活，此外还有碑碣、羊虎、纸钱、石鼓等名物的讲说，缘此常为研究唐代文化之所取材。

注解10：《易经》，《易经》是我国一部最古老而深邃的经典，据说是由伏羲的言论加以总结与修改概括而来（同时产生了易经八卦图），是华夏五千年智慧与文化的结晶，被誉为"群经之首，大道之源"。从本质上来讲，《易经》是一本关于"卜筮"之书。"卜筮"就是对未来事态的发展进行预测，而《易经》便是总结这些预测的规律理论的书。

注解11：《水浒传》，又名《忠义水浒传》，一般简称《水浒》，作于元末明初，是中国历史上第一部用白话文写成的章回小说，是我国四大名著之一。

注解12：赑屃：龙之九子之一，又名霸下。形似龟，好负重，长年累月驮载着石碑。人们在庙院祠堂里，处处可以见到这位任劳任怨的大力士。据说触摸它能给人带来福气。

注解13：《陪都纪略》，同治十二年，奉天（沈阳）刘世英所著《陪都纪略》，对研究沈阳的历史文化有很大价值，书中内容广博，对杂技和宫廷舞蹈等都有记载。

注解14：《何氏沈阳纪程》，作者何汝霖，字雨人，道光九年随驾东巡至沈阳起八月十八日迄十月二十三日往还，此书即其途中日记。

注解15：《沈故》，清同治年间的举人杨同桂著，卷端署"通州杨同桂伯馨辑"。杨同桂，字伯馨，顺天府通州（今北京通县）人，性警敏，学多有涉。东三省练兵大臣以年番阅，同桂来行营，历充帮办、奉天支应局总理、发审营务总办兼署翼长。后历充总理吉林边务粮饷处发审帮办、《吉林通志》提调兼分纂。光绪二十年（1894年）署长春知府，才干过人，颇得人心，撰有《沈故》、《吉林舆地略》、《吉林舆地图说》。

注解16：整牛供，牛煮熟后，将其头、尾、脊及四蹄放在俎内，是为"整牛供"。

注解17：雉堞，雉，城墙。堞dié，城墙上齿状的矮墙。又称垛墙，上有垛口，可射箭和瞭望。内侧矮墙称为女墙，无垛口，以防兵士往来行走时跌下。

注解18：礓磜三路，礓磜即台阶。

注解19：筐，圆形的竹筐。

注解20：七大恨：七大恨是努尔哈赤发布的讨明檄文。天命三年（万历四十六年，1618年）正月，努尔哈赤对诸贝勒宣布："吾意已决，今岁必征大明国！"，四月十三日以"害我祖父；逞兵越界，卫助叶赫；俾我已聘之女，改适蒙古；遗书诟言，肆行凌辱……"等七大恨告天，起兵反明。

注解21：一女灭四国，东哥的叔叔纳林布禄先后把她许了几个婆家，包括努尔哈赤，阿巴亥的叔父乌拉部的布占泰，哈达部的猛格布禄，她待嫁二十年，最后在三十三岁时嫁给了蒙古援兔的儿子吉赛，婚后不到一年就死了。努尔哈赤以悔婚夺婚为借口，一举灭了海西女真四部，这就是一女灭四国的由来。

注解22：佛八宝，即所谓法螺、法轮、宝伞、白盖、莲花、宝罐、圣鱼、盘肠的纹饰。

注解23：暗八仙，即汉钟离的温凉扇、曹国舅的阴阳板、吕洞宾的宝剑、韩湘子的横笛、铁拐李的葫芦、何仙姑的荷花、蓝采和的花篮以及张果老的渔鼓。

注解24：国语骑射："国语"即满语，在清代又叫"清语"；骑射即能在骑马奔驰中射中前的靶心，它是满族长期狩猎生活中的民族特技。清初考核八旗成员的起码要求是，自幼即当学习"国语骑射"，直至六十岁以上方能免试。不但八旗中的满、蒙成员必须能以满语奏对履历，能在马背上奔驰骑射，就是对汉军成员也不例外。

注解25：自来石，所谓"自来石"，是一根人工凿成的汉白玉石条，是古代墓室门常设的一种机关。自来石会自动将墓门封死的原理是，先将墓门门轴的上下端制作成球状，又在两扇墓门中间齐门缝的相同部位，雕凿出一个表面突起的槽，然后再在门内中轴线不远的石铺地面上，凿出一个前浅后深的槽来。关闭墓门前，人们先将石条，放在地面的凹槽内，并慢慢让其前倾，使之与墓门接触。当人们从地宫中撤出后，石条借助其本身倾斜的压力和门轴轴端的"滚珠"作用，自动地推着墓门关闭，直到它的顶端落在两扇墓门的那个凸槽内。这时，若要从外面将墓门推开，只能是痴心妄想。

NOTES

Note 1: This phrase is from "Yung Yey" of Analects of Confucius, "the wise take pleasures in streams; the benevolent find pleasures in hills. The wise are active; the benevolent are tranquil. The wise are joyful; the benevolent are long-lived." The wise are logical and good at dealing with affairs, like water flowing without obstacles, so the wise take pleasures in streams. The benevolent have firm faith in righteousness, which is as still as hills, and nothing can change it, therefore the benevolent find pleasure in hills. Some employ "Five Elements" theory to interpret it, according to which, "the wise possess the characteristic of earth, so they can take pleasures from water; the benevolent possess the characteristic of wood, so they can find pleasures from hills." The controversial pronunciations of three Chinese character " 乐 " in Confucius' words also poses questions for a long time. It is certain that pronunciations of the first two are same, but some think they are pronounced as "yao", others say they are pronounced as "yue." The third one is prounounced as "le" as in Modern Chinese, which delivers its basic meaning.

Note 2: Huangdi Mausoleum: also Mausoleum of Emperor Yellow, whose name is Xuanyuan, founder of Chinese Nation. According to folk stories, Huangdi has ascended into heaven because of his noble virtues, so his mausoleum is a cenotaph. It stands at top of Mount Qiao, north of Huangling County in Shaan'xi Province. In 1961, the State Council designated the mausoleum to be one of the earliest key historical sites under state protection, numbering it the "No. 1 Ancient Tomb," which therefore is also titled as "The No. 1 Mausoleum." I visited Huangdi Mausoleum in 2005 when I participated in Yan'an Planning Program.

Yandi Mausoleum: There are three altogether, including "Yandi Mausoleum of Yanling County in Hunan Province," "Yandi Mausoleum of Baoji City in Shaan'xi Province" and "Yandi Mausoleum of Gaoping City, Shanxi Province." In order to study Chinese advertising history, I went to Yandi Mausoleum of Baoji in 2005.

Dayu Mausoleum: It stands outside a temple gate of Mount Ji, three kilometers away from Shaoxing City. It is a large-scale classical building complex, which is made up of tombs, ancestral hall and temple. It covers more than 40 mu (a traditional unit of area, equaling to 0.0667 hectare or 1/6 acre), with the building area more than 2,700 square meters, It has been listed as a key historical site under state protection. I visited Dayu Mausoleum in 2005 with the purpose of studying Chinese advertising history.

Shaohao Mausoleum: In order to study Chinese advertising history, I have been to many mausoleums, among which Shaohao Mausoleum is also one of my destinations in that period. Shaohao, son of Huangdi, founded a capital city in Qiongsang, and afterwards moved to Qufu. He reigned there for 84 years, died at age one hundred years, and was buried at Shouqiu, east of the ancient capital of Lu Kingdom, which is at the northeast of Jiuxian village, four kilometers away from Qufu City. The mausoleum is 28.5 meters wide and 8.73 meters high, with its peak 12 meters high. With the shape of a pyramid, it is called as "pyramid of China."

Qin Shihuang Mausoleum: I went there in 1991 when I did my research work on Chinese advertising history. Qin Shihuang is the first emperor of Qin Dynasty, among which "shi" means "begin" or "the first", and "huang" means "emperor." It stands at the foot of Mount Li, to the east of Lintong County, which is over 30 kilometers away from Xi'an City. According to historical records, Qin Shihuang began to build his mausoleum since he came to the throne when he was 13 years old. The mausoleum was designed by his Prime Minister Li Si, and its construction was supervised by his General Zhang Han. The construction of the building lasted 38 years. This great project of grandeur has led to the fashion of lavish funerals among Chinese feudal rulers.

Han Wudi Mausoleum: Han Wudi refers to Emperor Wu of Han Dynasty, whose name is Liu Che. He is a feudal monarch with resourcefulness comparable to Qinshihuang. His mausoleum stands at Maoling Village, northeast of Xingping City (original Xingping County), which is 40 kilometers to the northwest of Xi'an City. The construction lasted 53 years from 139 B. C. to 87 B. C. It is now a key historical site under state protection. I visited Han Wudi Mausoleum twice respectively in 1996 and 2005 with the purpose of studying Chinese advertising history.

Guangwudi Mausoleum: It is built for Eastern Han Dynasty Emperor Liuxiu (6 B. C. – 57 A. D.), courtesy named Wenshu, born in Caiyang of Nanyang (southwest of Zaoyang in Hubei Province today), the ninth grandson of Emperor Gaozu. The mausoleum was also called as Liuxiu Tomb, and it stands around Tiexie Village of Mengjin County in Henan Province. It has Mount Mang at its back and faces the Yellow River to the north. It is a big grave mound, 1400 meters in perimeter and 20 meters high. More than one thousand ancient cypresses grow here, tall and sturdy, shady and quiet. I paid a visit to Guangwudi Mausoleum when I lectured in Yingyang, Henan Province in 2004.

Tang Taizong Mausoleum: Tang Taizong, Emperor Taizong of Tang Dynasty, whose name is Li Shimin, is the second emperor in Tang Dynasty. His mausoleum is called Zhaoling Imperial Tomb, the same as that of Emperor Hong Taiji, founder of Qing Dynasty. TangZhaoling Imperial Tomb is the largest mausoleum among "Eighteen Mausoleums of Tang" in central Shaan'xi

Plain of Shaan'xi Province, which stands on Mount Jiuzong, 22.5 kilometer to the northeast of Liquan County in Shaan'xi province. I went to TangZhaoling Imperial Tomb on my graduation tour in 1991.

Tang Gaozong and Wu Zetian Mausoleum: Wu Zetian is the only empress in China's history, also the oldest one that came to the throne (67 years old) and the longest living of all emperors (82 years old). She had been the empress of Tang Ggaozong (Emperor Gaozong of Tang Dynasty), and Queen Mother in the periods of Tang Zhongzong (Emperor Zhongzong of Tang Dynasty) and Tang Ruizong (Emperor Ruizong of Tang Dynasty). Later she titled herself as Emperor Wuzhou, changed Tang into Zhou, and moved her capital to Luoyang. Her monarch is historically called "Wuzhou" or "Nanzhou." She gave up the throne in 705 A.D. After she died, she requested to be buried with Tang Gaozong. Her mausoleum lies in Qian County of Xi'an, therefore also called Qian Mausoleum. It is the only mausoleum in the world that accommodates two emperors of two dynasties who were a couple. It was built in 684 A.D. and took 23 years to be completed. I went to the Mausoleum on my graduation tour in 1991, whose Wordless Memorial Tablet in Qian Mausoleum left a deep impression in my mind.

Song Taizu, Zhaokuangyin Mausoleum: Zhao Kuangyin (927 – 976), first emperor of Song Dynasty, was born in Zhuozhou (Zhuo County of Hebei Province today). He had held the posts of Head Detective Inspector of Later Zhou Dynasty and military governor of Songzhou. In 960 A.D., he took the throne by starting a military mutiny at Chenqiao. Then, he changed the nation's title to Song, founded Song Dynasty, and set his capital in Kaifeng, Henan Province. He died in 976, and was buried in Mausoleum Area of Song. His mausoleum is named as Yong Chang. I visited Yongchang Mausoleum when I lectured in Gongyi of Henan Province in 2005.

Song Shenzong, Zhao Xu's Mausoleum: Zhao Xu, Emperor Shenzong of Song Dynasty, was "studious and inquisitive, forgetting to eat late in a day." When he was a prince, he liked reading military works of Han Feizi. His reigning period is from 1067 to 1085. After he died, he was buried in Yongyu Mausoleum, which was built in 1085. The stone carvings of his mausoleum are the representative works during the late period of Song mausoleums. Its modeling of stone lion and carving craftsmanship rank first among all the carvings in Song mausoleums. It is commented, "Dongling's lion, Xiling's elephant, Good stone ship in the river of Hutuo." I visited Yongchang Mausoleum to see stone inscription there when I lectured in Gongyi of Henan Province in 2005.

Song Zhezong, Zhaoxu Mausoleum: Zhao Xu (1076—1100), Song Zhezong, the 6th son of Emperor Shenzong, the 7th emperor of Northern Song Dynasty, whose original name is Yong, had been entitled King of Yan'an. Yongtai Mausoleum lies in the south of Baling Village of Zhitian Town in Gong County, four miles away from Zhitian in the northeastern direction. 400 meters away from Yongyu Mausoleum. Yongyu Mausoleum has been destroyed many times by Jin Dynasty, the cruelest of which is Song Zhezong's skeleton was strewn randomly out of the Mausoleum. Later his subordinates collected the bones, wrapped them up and placed it back again. Now there is only one earthen mound left. I visited this mausoleum together with other two Song mausoleums when I lectured in Gongyi of Henan Province.

Genghis Khan's Mausoleum: Genghis Khan's Mausoleum lies on Prairie of Ejin Horo Banner in Erdos of Inner Mongolia, 70 kilometers away from Dongsheng District. "Secret Burial" is popular among Mongolian, therefore, nobody knows where Genghis Khan's tomb lies. The current tomb of his is only a cenotaph. After being removed many times, it finally returned to its hometown, Ejin Horo Banner from Kumbum of Huangzhong County, 185 kilometers away from Baotou in the northern direction. I visited the Mausoleum in 1997 when I lectured in Naiman Banner of Inner Mongolia. It's already 14 years from then on.

Ming Xiao Mausoleum: Ming Xiao Mausoleum is located at the west of Mount Mao, and the foot of Wanzhu Hill of Dulongfu to the southern side of Mount Zhijin (also Mount Zhong) in the east of Nanjing. The founding Emperor of Ming Dynasty, Zhu Yuanzhang, was buried here with his Empress. It is one of the largest ancient emperors' mausoleums existing, which bears characteristics of Tang and Song Dynasties and other previous mausoleums, which were built upon mountains. Later by transforming rectangular tombs into circular mounds, he started a new layout of mausoleums with features of "rectangular in the front and round in the back." I paid a visit to this mausoleum in 1996 when I lectured for Nanjing Panda Electronics.

Thirteen Tombs of Ming Dynasty: Here are group tombs for emperors of Ming Dynasty, which obtained the name for burying thirteen emperors. They are located in Tianshou Hill of Mount Yan inside Changping District in the northwest suburb of Beijing. From May of the 7th year of Yongle (1407) when Chang Mausoleum began to be built to Si Mausoleum was completed for the last emperor Chongzhen, 13 mausoleums had been built within a period of more than 230 years, together with 7 tombs for concubines, 1 tomb for court eunuch. Here are buried 13 emperors, 23 empresses, 2 princes, over 30 concubines, and 1 eunuch. I accompanied my parents for outing to Thirteen Tombs of Ming Dynasty in 1998.

Note 3: Dragon Vein: Nurhaci and his descendants believed that the imperial power of Later Jin Dynasty and Great Qing Dynasty originated from Mount Changbai, which runs from northeast to southwest and divides into Mount Qiao, where Old Hetuala City is located, and Mount Hui of Shenyang. These two mountain ridges are called "Dragon Vein," also called "Dragon Ridge," which is thought to be imperial foundation of Qing Dynasty.

Note 4: Chronicles of Hong Taiji: On January 8th of lunar calendar, the 6th ruling year (1649) of Emperor Shunzhi, Qing Court ordered to compile Chronicles of Hong Taiji. Grand academicians Fan Wencheng, Gang Lin, Qi Chongge, Hong Chengchou, Feng Quan, Ning Wanwo, Song Quan worked as general directors, and academicians Wang Duo, Zha Buhai as assistant directors.

Note 5: Records of Qing Dynasty: Its full name is Veritable Records of Great Qing through all Reign Periods, a chronologically arranged collection of facts of Qing Dynasty with a total amount of 4,484 volumes. It is a collection of imperial edicts, memorials to throne, emperor's daily life, wedding, funeral, sacrifice and other miscellaneous activities like inspection touring, concubine picking, with articles varied in number and length through 12 reigns. The contents of the records through different reigns vary slightly, but the categories are mainly the same covering politics, economics, culture, military, diplomacy, and natural phenomena, and many other aspects.

Note 6: Heitu Records: the records of Qing Dynasty General Imperial Household Department of Shengjing are the official correspondences between General Imperial Household Department of Shengjing and General Imperial Household Department of Beijing, Shengjing General, Mukden Governor, Five Departments of Shengjing, recording the detailed activities of royal family and imperial court affairs, which are the valuable resources for the study of the local political and economic situations in Northeast and the role of Shengjing in Qing Dynasty.

Note 7: Lingxing: also called Ling Star or Tiantian Star, which was supposed to be sacrificed first when offering sacrifices to God of Heaven for good harvest, under the stipulation of Emperor Gaozu, founder of Han Dynasty. In Song Dynasty, the rites for God were adopted to pay respect to Confucius, and later 棂星 (Ling Xing) was rewritten as 櫺星 (Ling Xing). What is Lingxing Gate? Lingxing was originally referred to as Wenxing, star of academicians in ancient astronomy, which symbolizes all men of letter gathering there. Lingxing Gates of Confucius Temples in both Nanjing and in Qufu are the first entrance to the temple.

Note 8: Pailou: "Lou" in Pailou refers to the parts of cockloft of the ridge roof, which can be divided into six categories: 1 cockloft, 3 cocklofts, 5 cocklofts, 7 cocklofts, 9 cocklofts and 11 cocklofts. Pailous can also be built with different number of bays, of which only odd numbers are accepted. Usually Pailous of 9 cocklofts are dedicated to emperors.

Note 9: Records of What Feng Saw and Heard consist of 10 volumes, written by Feng Yan in Tang Dynasty. This book enjoys a high historical resource value, with very organized layout. It contains one hundred themes with each theme summarized in two Chinese characters, such as Taoism, Confucianism, writing, Imperial Examination. The book covers a wide range of topics. It includes political systems like imperial examination, official election; official practices of wall tablet record, tail burning; social life like wedding ceremony, clothing, food, ball playing, tug of war, rope skills; and others like introduction to and explanation of steles, stone sheep and tiger, paper money, stone drum, which are therefore ideal resources for the study of the cultures of Tang Dynasty.

Note 10: Book of Change: The book is the most ancient and profound classic, reportedly summarized from Fu Xi's remarks (which simultaneously evolved Eight Trigrams), which is crystallizations of wisdoms and cultures of Chinese history for the last five thousand years, known as "Masterpiece of masterpieces, fountain of knowledge." In essence, Book of Change is a book on "divination," which is prediction of future developments, and Book of Change is the summary of these prediction theories.

Note 11: Water Margins: The book is also entitled as Outlaws of the Marsh, a first novel in the form of chapter written in vernacular language in Chinese history. It was completed in the late Yuan and early Ming Dynasties, and it is one of Four Great Famous Classic Novels in China.

Note 12: Bixi: one of nine sons of King Dragon, also known as Baxia (霸下). It looks like a turtle in shape, good at weight-bearing, so it carries a huge stone tablet on its back over years. People can see this sculpture everywhere in monastic and ancestral temples. It is said that touching it can bring us good fortune.

Note 13: Memoirs of Shengjing: The book was written in Mukden (Shenyang) by Liu Shiying in the 12th ruling year of Emperor Tongzhi, which covers extensive fields such as acrobatics, royal dance, and is of great value for the study of history and culture of Shenyang.

Note 14: Travel Notes to Shenyang: This book was written by He Rulin, with the style of Yuren (rainman), which is a diary on his way to and back from Shenyang while accompanying Emperor to travel eastwards from August 18th to October 23rd in the 9th ruling year of Emperor Daoguang.

Note 15: Shengu: This book was authored by Yang Tonggui, a provincial graduate in the reign of Emperor Tongzhi in Qing Dynasty. On top of the volume reads "By Yang Tonggui, styled as Boxin from Tongzhou." Yang Tonggui, Yang Boxin as his style, born in Tongzhou (Tong County in Beijing now) in Shuntian Prefecture, was a clever and learned man with profound knowledge. There was annual inspection of soldier training in the three provinces in northeast China. Yang Tonggui came to field headquarters and worked as deputy chief, director of Mukden Special Financial Bureau, financial supervision chief and deputy governor. Later he worked as financial supervision deputy chief in Jilin Army Provision Bureau, coordinator and assistant editor of Overall History of Jilin. In the 20th ruling year of Emperor Guangxu (1894), he was entitled prefect of Changchun because of his extraordinary talents and reputation. He is author of Shengu, Jilin Geography Survey, Jilin Geographical Maps.

Note 16: Entire Cattle Sacrifice: After being cooked thoroughly, the cattle's head, tail, backbone and four hooves are displayed on riyual vessels for sacrifices, which is hence called Entire Cattle Sacrifice.

Note 17: Zhidie (battlement): "Zhi" means city wall; "Die" means crenelations on city wall, also called Duoqiang, through which soldiers could watch and shoot arrows. Parapet wall refers to the wall inside without crenelations, used to prevent soldiers from falling down.

Note 18: Three way Jiangca: "Jiangca" means steps.

Note 19: "Fei" refers to round bamboo basket.

Note 20: Seven Hatreds: This is an official denunciation of Ming Dynasty issued by Nurhaci. In January of the third ruling year of Tianming (also the 46th ruling year of Emperor Wanli of Ming Dynasty, i.e. 1618), Nurhaci announced to his Baylors, "I have made my decision that I will conquer Ming this year!" On April 13, he declared the war against Ming with 7 hatreds he claimed, which are "killing my grandfather; crossing borders and helping Yehe tribe; looking down upon Manchu and remarrying Lady Dongge to Mongolia; criticizing and suppressing Manchu."

Note 21: One woman ruined four kingdoms. Dongge's uncle, Nalinbulu, promised a number of families to marry his niece, including Nurhaci, Buzhantai in Ural tribe of Abbahai's uncle, and Menggebulu in Hada tribe. Dongge waited to be married for twenty years, and at the age of 33, she married Jisai, son of Mongolian Shoutu, but died less than a year after her marriage. Nurhaci took the breach of Marriage Engagement as pretext and conquered the four tribes of Jurchen. This is the origin of "One woman ruined four kingdoms."

Note 22: Eight Buddhist Emblems: They are identified as patterns of divine conch, divine wheel, divine umbrella, white canopy, lotus, divine pot, Saint fish, winding intestinal.

Note 23: Covert Eight Immortals: They refer to eight magical tools used by Eight Immortals, including Han Zhongli's fan, Royal Uncle Cao's yin and yang board, Lü Dongbin's sword, Philosopher Han Xiang's fife, Iron-Crutch Li's gourd, Immortal Lady He's lotus, Lan Caihe's flower basket, and Elder Zhang Guo's fishing drum. Eight Immortals are traditional legendary figures in Taoist mythology.

Note 24: National Language and Riding-shooting: "National language" refers to Manchu language, also known as "Qing language," in the Qing Dynasty. Riding-shooting means to shoot the bull's eye with arrows while riding, which is a special skill for Manchu people to gain in their traditional hunting life. The minimum requirement for assessment of Bannermen in early Qing Dynasty was that they must learn their "national language and riding-shooting" from childhood. Only those who were above 60 years old could be exempted from examination. Manchu and Mongolian members in the Eight Banners must be able to speak fluent Manchu language, and shoot while riding on horsebacks, without exception of Hanmembers in their army.

Note 25: Auto-sliding Stone. The so-called "auto-sliding stone" is a man-made white marble bar, a tool used to lock tomb entrance in ancient times. Mechanism of auto-sliding stone to lock tomb entrance is as follows: cut two ends of door axes into ball-shaped shafts, cut out a projecting groove above surface in the middle of two doors, and then carve a slope slot on the stone ground on the frame axis not far from the doors. Before tomb doors are closed, the stone bar should put in the slot and let it lean against tomb doors. The tomb doors are pushed to slide until stone bar fall in the projecting groove with their own weight exerting on the door and the turning mechanism of shafts, thus tomb doors are closed. Now, it's impossible to open tomb doors from outside of the tomb.

图书在版编目（CIP）数据

福陵／赵琛著．—北京：中国建筑工业出版社，
2011.11
（世界文化遗产　辽宁卷）
ISBN 978-7-112-13710-7

Ⅰ.①福… Ⅱ.①赵… Ⅲ.①陵墓－概况－沈阳市－
清前期 Ⅳ.①K928.76

中国版本图书馆CIP数据核字（2011）第213314号

译　　者：黄　皓　李连涛

责任编辑：吴　绫
责任设计：叶延春
责任校对：陈晶晶　赵　颖

世界文化遗产　辽宁卷
福　陵
WORLD HERITAGE　LIAONING VOLUME
FULING IMPERIAL TOMB
赵琛　著
*
中国建筑工业出版社出版、发行（北京西郊百万庄）
各地新华书店、建筑书店经销
北京锋尚制版有限公司制版
北京盛通印刷股份有限公司印刷
*
开本：965×1270毫米　1/16　印张：11　字数：428千字
2011年12月第一版　2011年12月第一次印刷
定价：128.00元
ISBN 978-7-112-13710-7
（21492）

版权所有　翻印必究
如有印装质量问题，可寄本社退换
（邮政编码　100037）